D0371678

DATE DUE

EVERYTHING WILL BE ALL RIGHT

EVERYTHING WILL BE ALL RIGHT

a memoir

DOUGLAS WALLACE

GREENLEAF
BOOK GROUP PRESS

Published by Greenleaf Book Group Press
Austin, TX
www.greenleafbookgroup.com

First edition published 2009 by D & P Press

Distributed by Greenleaf Book Group LLC

For ordering information or special discounts for bulk purchases, please contact
Greenleaf Book Group LLC at PO Box 91869, Austin, TX 78709, (512) 891-6100.

Design and composition by Greenleaf Book Group LLC
Cover design by Greenleaf Book Group LLC

Publisher's Cataloging-In-Publication Data
(Prepared by The Donohue Group, Inc.)

Wallace, Douglas (Douglas Wayne), 1949-
  Everything will be all right : a memoir /-- Douglas Wallace. -- 2nd ed.

    p. ; cm.

  Second ed. of: Everything will be all right. D & P Press, 2009.
  ISBN: 978-1-60832-004-2

1. Wallace, Douglas (Douglas Wayne), 1949- 2. Lawyers--Tennessee--Biography. I.
Title.

KF373.W35 A3 2009
349/.092 B   2009925254

Part of the Tree Neutral™ program, which offsets the number of trees consumed in
the production and printing of this book by taking proactive steps, such as planting
trees in direct proportion to the number of trees used: www.treeneutral.com

TreeNeutral

Printed in the United States of America on acid-free paper

09 10 11 12 13 14   10 9 8 7 6 5 4 3 2 1

Second Edition

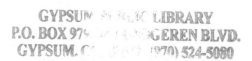

To victims of poverty around the world:
I pray that the light of love and peace will shine upon
you and that you will find the courage to persevere
and prevail in your search for a way out.

Acknowledgments

My deepest gratitude goes to my children, Laura, Russell, and Cindy for their encouragement. A special acknowledgement goes to my mother for all the time spent going over the details and stories of the early year. This book could not have been written without the countless hours of support from my adoring wife Peggy. Special recognition goes to Stephen Hawley, a friend, teacher, and author whose advice was invaluable.

Preface

I t has been said that those born into poverty remain enchained in an endless cycle of poverty. This was true for both of my parents. This book is about how I broke the chain.

I am a child of the rural South. I grew up in a series of small towns and in the backwoods of upstate Tennessee. I was the third oldest of eight children—six boys and two girls. Our father spent most of his life drinking, raging, and drifting from job to job. Our mother was a battered wife who held the family together with ferocious love and weary grit. We lived like itinerants. We subsisted at the very bottom, invisibly, among those members of society whose voices go unheard or have been silenced. Finding my own voice—freeing that choked spring within—remains an ongoing challenge for me.

There's nothing good about poverty. It can steal your life away. It isolates you, degrades your sense of self-worth, renders you a third-class citizen; it leaves you feeling incomplete, and threatens your very survival. I was born at home in one of the most beautiful parts of the country, surrounded by hills and trees as far as the eye could see. But I was also born into bone-crushing poverty—a hopeless lack of money, year in and year out, with no reason to believe it would get any better. From my earliest memory, I felt the constant stress of being poor, as do all children and teenagers growing up in poverty. As the impoverished grow into adulthood, they may settle for lives of quiet desperation. Or all that stress might explode in ways that bring painful consequences. Over many years, I've watched dear friends and beloved family members, one by one, allow poverty to pull them under, allow the shame to diminish them when there is no reason for shame. I've seen them allow addiction to draw them away from any real solutions. As a boy, as soon as I was old enough to articulate it to myself, I was determined to not ever let this happen to me. I didn't.

My story is about how I was able to overcome the odds. It includes good choices, bad choices, and hard choices; wrong turns, right turns, and dead ends; violent and nonviolent encounters. I've written this book to make sense of my life, to put some demons to rest, and, if possible, to help anyone struggling to find their way.

One of the blessings of starting out with nothing is that practically every person, every situation, and every encounter becomes your teacher—at least that's how it was and continues to be for me. I consider myself very fortunate in this. The teacher or the teachings can be cruel or kind, but the lesson is always valuable. For example, when I was eight years old, I experienced the ridicule of my third-grade classmates who laughed when I, the poorest kid in the school aside from my older brother and sister, dared to say that I wanted to be a lawyer when I grew up. The school principal backed them up and gave me my first taste of the low expectations—or no expectations—society holds for the poor. It was a defining, life-changing moment for me, for which I am now grateful. It ignited determination. It motivated me. From that moment on, rather than collapsing, my dream of becoming a lawyer crystallized. It became real, a true goal for my life. And I did, indeed, end up becoming a lawyer, a lawyer with my own firm, successful enough to enable me to retire at the age of fifty with financial independence.

Knowing what I wanted to do in that aspect of my life gave me a star to steer by, however wobbly at times. My mother, by the power of her example, fostered in me the strength to persevere, not perish, no matter what. Also, my life would have been a completely different life, I am convinced, had I not had a belief in a power greater than myself—both to guide me and to sustain me. When I was a boy, I had a spiritual experience that altered the course of my life profoundly and permanently, and which I write about in this book. The philosopher William James talks about several kinds of spiritual experience. Some come to a person slowly, over time; others—which are rarer—come more suddenly. Mine came more suddenly and ineffably. In all this time, it has been an impossibly difficult task to try to put this experience into words. Imagine an undeniable inner voice saying to you, deeply and tenderly, "Everything will be all right. Everything *is* all right. *You* are all right." This is the closest I can come to translating the profound undercurrent of inner peace upon which my entire life now rests. Sometimes it's stronger than others, but it's always there for me, and I believe this possibility exists in everyone.

As you read my story, you'll come upon many times when I've skated off track, been terribly afraid or depressed, or lacked confidence. It was my unwavering faith in the mantra-like message "Everything will be all right" that enabled me, time and again, to keep going.

Over the years, friends and acquaintances have urged me to put my story down on paper, and the book you hold in your hands is the result. I've written it with the hope that it might serve as an inspiration. My story proves that those born into discouraging circumstances are not destined to remain there. Whether we are poor materially or spiritually, I believe we each have choices. I believe that positive action is always possible and failure never inevitable. I also believe that help lies all around us, if only we are willing to see it and open ourselves to it.

PART ONE
Stewart County

CHAPTER ONE

Without Hard Work You Will Not Survive

U nder the scorching sun of a Tennessee summer, four barefoot children labored in a large, deep-green tobacco field ripe for cutting. Conditions were harsh. The steamy air was thick with gnats, the rocky soil bruised their naked feet, and the sticky tobacco leaves rubbed constantly against their sweating bodies. Dressed alike in denim overalls, the children were indistinguishable as they worked, crouched over the crop. Each wore a wide-brimmed straw hat, pulled down low against the boiling sun and the occasional wind that gusted through the hollow. Suddenly, one of the group stood upright and trained her keen blue eyes on the empty dirt road that bordered the field. The girl was ten years old and tall for her age, and she gripped the wooden handle of her hoe with young hands already made strong from working the land. Her face was camouflaged with brown tobacco stains, but fine-featured and *now intent with anticipation. She'd heard the distinct sound of the traveling peddler's wagon. She was sure of it. She stood motionless, waiting, listening, until the unmistakable clanging of pots and pans grew louder and there was no doubt.*

The tall girl dropped the hoe and began running, her two brothers and younger sister joining her in the footrace to the house, the peddler's horse-drawn wagon just rounding the bend. Weeks had gone by since the girl's father had promised her a new pair of shoes, and even longer since the peddler's last visit. But the day had finally arrived. In her mind's eye, she saw a pair of shining white shoes with long golden laces. The peddler would surely have them. With great expectation, she asked to see his selection, which she then looked over carefully. No white pair of girls' shoes was among his stock, with or without golden laces. To ease the huge disappointment, the girl's father suggested she instead buy a black pair, patent-leather shiny with stylishly pointed toes. These would look very nice on her, he said. But, with as much grace as she could gather, she declined the offer and, resolute, returned to the fields. The peddler slowly went on his way.

This girl was my mother. She told me later that she preferred having no shoes at all to accepting second best. My mother was born in 1925 to a sharecropping family on thirty-five acres of farmland and woods in the remote area of Cub Creek in Stewart County, Tennessee. Typically, sharecropping involves rich landowners and very poor tenant farmers. But in Stewart County, pretty much everyone was poor, even the landlord, although he was a bit less so. Between the landless and the landed, poor was a matter of degree. Almost no one was living well or handsomely.

Generations of Gregorys lived as sharecroppers in Stewart County. My mother's father, Ellis Gregory, my grandfather, was a sharecropper just like his father before him, and his father before him. He was a farmer without a farm, a man with few resources. He could not read or write, nor could my grandmother, Mavis Gregory. The family lived season to season, always one tobacco crop away from slipping into a maw of crushing debt. Tobacco seasons were never predictable. Even at the end of a successful season, rarely did the family clear enough money to tide them over for the year. The family became practiced at getting by on next to nothing.

Tobacco requires a tremendous amount of arduous hand labor. All eight of the Gregory children—Ralph, Ardell, my mother Eunice, Elmer, Virgil, Wesley, Lois, and Eva—went to work in the fields as soon as they were old enough to lift a hoe, which was usually around age six or seven. During the blazing hot summers, the children worked from sunup to sundown; during the school year, from the time they got home from school until dark.

They attended a one-room schoolhouse a mile away. One by one, each dropped out before reaching middle school—my mother after finishing fifth grade—to work full-time on the farm. The survival of the family depended on it. Each and every year, the Gregorys had one primary objective: producing tobacco and getting it to market.

The annual cycle of a tobacco crop would begin in late winter, February or March, when a mule team plowed the plant beds that would later be sown with tobacco seed. Throughout the spring, the seeds sprouted and developed into young plants, and the mule team continued to plow the crop ground. By late spring, the young tobacco plants were ready to be transplanted from the plant beds to the furrowed fields. There they developed into mature tobacco plants throughout the summer, three long months of continual hoeing, worming, topping, and suckering. When a tobacco plant is half-grown, flower buds appear. These flower buds are then removed or "topped" to prevent seed formation and to stimulate leaf production. The desired result is a larger, thicker, darker leaf that matures uniformly and contains more nicotine.

Topping must be done by hand, one plant at a time. For my mother and her family, this required two or three trips over each of the many fields to ensure the removal of all the flower buds. Following topping is suckering, the most labor-intensive activity in tobacco cultivation. While topping cultivates a better leaf, it also stimulates the undesirable growth of secondary stems, known as suckers. These, too, need to be removed to ensure uniformity and the highest-quality plant. My mother said that most days there was so much work it seemed like they would never see the end of it.

By the end of summer, the plants ripened into full, healthy, deep, green leaves—some as wide as fifteen inches—and were ready for harvest. Each individual plant had to be cut at the base of the stalk, the stalks bundled onto wooden stakes, and the staked bundles hung from the rafters inside the tobacco barn, a dangerous task. The tobacco was then cured inside the barn by "firing." On the dirt floor, a smoldering fire of hickory or oak burned at a hundred-degree heat. Keeping the heat constant was my grandfather's responsibility, with the children in assistance. The intense smoke inside the barn would burn their eyes. Too little heat, the tobacco gets moldy; too much heat, the barn burns down. My grandfather would have to stay with it, sometimes all night long.

By late December or early January, the crop would be ready for market, the Gregory family's yearlong effort concluded. The cured leaves had been stripped from their stalks, tied into six- to ten-leaf bundles, and loaded onto mule-driven wagons to take to the town of Clarksville, about twenty miles away. If they were fortunate, the Gregorys' share of the harvest income would be enough to pay off the bills accumulated over the year, with a little extra to put aside for the coming months. My grandmother put any surplus cash in a cloth tobacco pouch kept pinned beneath her clothes. In those days, families in Stewart County had no use for banks.

The children were taught a single guiding principle for life: without work, without *hard* work, you will not survive. My grandfather's work ethic was as much a force of nature in the family's life as the suffocating heat of summer and the intense, icy cold of winter. My grandfather Gregory was a highly self-disciplined, formidable man, six feet two, lean and hard-bodied, with high cheekbones and heavy dark eyebrows that overhung piercing deep-set eyes. And he was strict.

He didn't believe in wasting daylight. A slight hesitation to obey his command was cause for a swift boot-kick to the rear or a switching with a hickory branch or even a horsewhip. As soon as they were old enough, everyone worked. No exceptions. My mother remembers one time, when her oldest brother refused to work in the tobacco field, my grandfather punched him in the face with his fist. For my grandfather, hard work was a matter of life and death. It was the only way he knew how to survive. This was my mother's childhood experience and education.

Like my mother, my father, Brady Wallace, was born and raised on a rural patch of farmland in the backwoods of Stewart County. He grew up in an area known to the locals as Potneck, which to this day appears on no map. Potneck sits on the northern bank of the seven-hundred-mile-long Cumberland River, which flows south from Kentucky, snakes through Tennessee, and then curves back up into Kentucky before draining into the Ohio River. Like so many places in the South, Potneck has several differing stories about how it got its name. One version attributes it to a crook in the river that resembles the neck of a teapot. Another from the 1800s refers to an alleged argument between a man living north of the river and a man living south of the river. The northsider smacked the southsider with a skillet, whereupon the southsider hit back with a pot that then broke at its neck. The spot to the south became known as Lick Skillet; the area to the north as Potneck.

My parents had other things in common. Each came from large families. My father's siblings were named Ora Grace, Merlene, Marcene, Pete, Cordell, and Edgar. Although they weren't sharecroppers, the Wallaces were also tobacco farmers and, like the Gregorys, lived crop to crop, season to season. My grandfather, Jim Wallace, owned a plot of five acres that had trickled down to him from his great-great-great-great-grandfather Wallace, who had received a land grant of three hundred acres as compensation for fighting as a soldier on the side of the Patriots—the Continental Army—in the American Revolution. The Wallaces were proud of being among the original settlers of Stewart County.

In Potneck, the Wallaces' small, wood-frame house was primitive, like the Gregorys', but it had an outhouse, electricity, and was owned outright. Set on old Potneck Road, the house was also less isolated. My brothers and sisters and I knew our paternal grandparents as Papa Jim and Mamma Pearl, and as a boy, I came to adore the Wallace side of the family. Many times they would come to our rescue.

Papa Jim had a fierce reputation as a man who protected his family at any cost. He was good-looking and broad shouldered, with light green eyes and dark brown skin. Sometimes people outside the family would call him "Black Jim" and kids at school would ask me if I was one of the "Black Wallaces." I remember asking my mother why people added "black" to our name. She explained it the way Papa Jim had always explained it: that he and some of the other Wallace family members were part Cherokee. Much later, as an adult, I learned the truth about Papa Jim's skin color: he was part African American. He wasn't the kind of man to conceal any part of his heritage. No doubt, his parents kept his black roots a secret in order to protect him.

Extreme racial prejudice abounded in Tennessee in those days. And in Stewart County, those Wallaces that were dark skinned were treated differently. This exclusion only drew them closer together as a family in common cause. The family was so tight-knit that, for a time, the Potneck community became synonymous with the Black Wallaces. Strangers entered Potneck at their own peril. But the Black Wallaces were not without a sense of humor about it all. One time, Papa Jim and a cousin played a joke on a lone stranger who had dared to enter Potneck in his Model T Ford unannounced. The oblivious stranger soon came upon two men, apparently dead, lying prone in the middle of the road. He stopped sharply and ran to the two bodies, when suddenly Papa Jim and his cousin bolted to their feet pointing twelve-gauge shotguns in the driver's face. The stranger sped off in the opposite direction to the howls of the Wallace boys' laughter.

In 1945, my mother met my father at a twenty-first birthday party given for him by Papa Jim and Mamma Pearl at the Potneck house. At five feet eight, my father was of medium height, strongly built, physically fit, and with a ready smile and shock of thick brown hair. My mother thought him handsome. He had dropped out of school after finishing the eighth grade, but wanted to get out of working the family's tobacco fields as soon as possible. So he had enrolled in the Civilian Conservation Corps, a government program designed back then to train poor and unskilled youths in a trade. He learned carpentry and, afterward, worked odd jobs around the county, including digging trenches and repairing old cars, especially those everyone else had given up on.

My father had a natural talent for seeing opportunity and solutions where others saw problems. He didn't see junk when he looked at an old beat-up car; he saw opportunity. He'd grab the car for pennies, fix it up or find others to do so, and sell it for a nice profit. He'd buy a goat for pennies, barbecue it using his own recipes, and then sell the meat in sandwiches or by the pound.

My father had loads of charm and plenty of daring. He and his brothers were the first generation of our family in Potneck to experience the thrill of driving as teenagers. They sped down the dirt roads in their fixed-up 1920s automobiles, my father often accelerating as he raced around the bends. On approach, depending upon the curve of the turn, he would drop his right or left wheels into the roadside ditch for leverage and then push on the gas. One day, he masterfully steered to a stop a brakeless car gaining velocity as it tore backward down a very steep hill. After that, his driving skills were legendary in Potneck.

My father had little formal education, but he was an intelligent man and was blessed with the gift of persuasion and the inborn ability to get along with people. He and my mother married shortly after his twenty-first birthday party. Things looked promising.

Though my mother was only twenty, my father was her second husband. Three years earlier, she had married a boy named Grady Hardie, who, feeling compelled to defend his country, had immediately enlisted in the United States Marine Corps when America entered World War II. He was sent to Okinawa, Japan, where he was killed in battle. Just a few months after her marriage, at age seventeen, my mother became a widow.

The United States government awarded her, as a war widow, a fifty-five-dollar monthly support check. It was a small fortune. The checks were guaranteed to continue until her first child reached age eighteen.

Just like my Grandmother Gregory, as long as a spot of land was available, however big or small, my mother planted a garden. She grew okra, squash, beans, potatoes, corn, tomatoes, and whatever else she had at hand. We would have fresh vegetables in the summer and she would preserve what she could for fall and winter.

Four years into her marriage with my father, in the sticky heat of midsummer and not far from Potneck, my mother was eight-and-a-half months pregnant with me and working barefoot in her garden. My two-year-old brother, Bracy, was playing on the ground nearby. My one-year-old sister, Faye, was settled contentedly on my mother's hip. With one arm wrapped around her baby girl, my mother was stooped over and weeding when her labor pains began. Straight away, she headed back to the house—one of a hundred sad, sunken shacks we would live in—still carrying Faye, with Bracy toddling behind. She took a shortcut past the well and through a patch of tall grass that hid a large piece of broken glass. The shard entered near the ball of her foot, piercing through completely to the other side. As blood gushed, she hobbled on one foot into the house and tried to collect herself. My father wasn't home and there was no way to contact him. They had no telephone; they had no car. She sat Faye down on the bare wood floor and began carefully to pull the glass from her foot. *God help me*, she thought.

"Bracy," she said calmly to her two-year-old. "Go get Aunt Lois." Lois was my mother's sister who lived just up the hill.

On his little legs Bracy ran barefoot all the way up the dirt road and brought Lois back with him. My mother was unquestionably in labor and the cut on her foot looked nasty.

"Eunice, you need a doctor!" Lois said.

"We don't have time for a doctor," my mother said. "Bracy, you know where Miss Dony lives. Now, you go get her for me."

Miss Dony was the midwife who lived a quarter-mile down the dirt road in the other direction. At age sixty, she had delivered many babies in her lifetime. For many of the local families, Miss Dony was the closest to a doctor they would ever have. She was highly knowledgeable in treating various injuries and diseases and, importantly, she offered her services for free.

From her front porch, Miss Dony heard the screams of the shirtless little boy as he came running toward her in the glaring July sun. As he drew closer, she recognized Bracy and remembered that his mother was pregnant. Grabbing her medical bag, she ran to meet the boy and together they rushed back down the unpaved road. Miss Dony found my mother in the final stages of labor. Immediately, she dressed the serious wound on my mother's foot and began making preparations for the delivery.

She encouraged my mother with the proverbial "push" and, soon afterward, she said, "Eunice, it's a boy child you got."

Douglas Wayne Wallace is the name my mother chose for me. In Stewart County, common practice was to use the middle name for everyday, so up until high school everybody called me Wayne. From high school on, I was known as Doug.

In those days, midwife deliveries weren't filed with the State of Tennessee. As a result, I wasn't issued a birth certificate. To this day there is no official record of my birth.

I was Eunice and Brady Wallace's third child. More would follow.

CHAPTER TWO

Poverty Keeps You Moving

After my parents got married, things did not go well for my father. His young family was expanding, a new baby just about every year. Odd jobs were scarce, full-time jobs scarcer. And he was having a hard time sticking with the jobs he managed to get. Rarely did we stay in one place for long. We lived in houses that rented for fifteen dollars a month. When we missed a payment, which was often, the landlord would usually allow us a grace period. But eventually, with the rent not forthcoming, he would tell us to move. Sometimes, we'd find a falling-down, vacant house and live there for a while, until we were found out and forced to move again.

Mom and Dad, for most of those early years, restricted our moving around to the sparse backwoods of Stewart County. No house we lived in stood farther than ten or fifteen miles from each other. To an adult, this would seem a small perimeter, but to a child, it was a vast expanse. For a long time, I had no idea where we were in relation to any place else. Our frequent and usually unannounced moves were more dislocations than relocations. We would land in a new place—rarely better than the last—not knowing how long it would be before we'd be gone again. Always, we traveled light. A single borrowed pickup truck would generally be sufficient for moving our few belongings. We didn't have permanent things. We had nothing holding us down. Perhaps my father preferred it that way, but it didn't work for the rest of us. We had no solid ground under us except for the Tennessee landscape that belonged to everyone, free and clear.

From as early as I can remember, I loved the out-of-doors and I loved the woods. The Tennessee hills, rivers, creeks, and deep woods were a natural playground for a boy. Stewart County was about as distant from material wealth as you could get, but its natural landscape was perfection.

In the summer of 1955, when I was six, Dad decided to move us two hundred and forty miles away to Granite City, Illinois.

Granite City had been home to heavy industry since the turn of the century. At that time, Granite City Steel, American Steel Founders, and other steel enterprises were hiring workers by the thousands, and people came from all over the country seeking good-paying jobs. Many Stewart County men had already made the trip to Granite City, including my paternal grandfather, although Papa Jim didn't stay.

Dad went on ahead to seek employment, while the rest of us—six kids by then—moved in temporarily with Papa Jim and Mamma Pearl to await word. It didn't take long. After a few weeks, money arrived from Granite City, along with instructions for making the trip. Dad was taking care of his family. Maybe we were going to be all right after all.

The Greyhound bus ride from Tennessee to Illinois was long, difficult, and hot. The main route north was old Highway 41, and the bus stopped at every small town along the way. At some of the larger towns, we had to disembark and transfer to another bus, with a wait of several hours in between. Mom had only a little money to feed all of us during the two-day trip. Also, at thirty years old, she'd never been on a bus before—nor had she ever been out of Tennessee—and wasn't aware that a restroom was on board. During the first day, the youngest among us had a few "accidents," causing some serious olfactory discomfort to the other passengers and perhaps to the bus driver as well. He pulled over to the side of the road, walked down the aisle to where Mom was sitting, and said, "Ma'am, do you know there's a restroom on this bus?"

Once in the restroom at the back of the bus, Mom washed and diapered the little ones, and then threw the soiled clothes out the restroom window.

When we arrived in Granite City, we reunited with Dad and moved directly into a subsidized public housing project known as Kirkpatrick Homes. Rows of dingy two-story brick and concrete buildings stretched for city blocks, a bleak tract of apartment buildings bordered by chain-link fencing and broken up only by pockmarked driveways and a few asphalt playgrounds. I don't remember any trees. Through the thin walls of our small apartment you could hear the neighbors quarrelling. We shared a front stoop with the family next door. A front lawn, barely fifteen feet wide and unkempt, was usually occupied with mothers and their children, sitting on blankets or folding metal chairs and seeking relief from the hot, claustrophobic apartments.

Mom often sat on the front steps talking with one of her new friends, while I'd sit on the grass nearby and listen to their stories. They spoke about their hardships both growing up and now. All the while, a bar across the street—Mom called it a juke joint—would blare songs like "Mister Sandman" by the Chordettes and "Rock Around the Clock" by Bill Haley and His Comets. After dark, the sounds of the neighborhood became even louder, and the bar would pump up the volume on the jukebox. Night after night, I remember trying to fall asleep to songs by Elvis or the first rock-and-roll bands.

I liked the music, but the overall noise and crowded conditions of the projects depressed me. I longed for the quiet and open spaces of the countryside back home.

That fall, I enrolled in school for the first time—in first grade. I remember feeling very afraid about going to Marshall Elementary, a large city school near the projects. There were hundreds of kids. The hallways seemed to go on forever. The high ceilings and rows of classroom doors made my legs feel watery. It must have been just as hard on Bracy and Faye, who'd only attended one-room school-houses back in Stewart County.

On my first day, I wanted to be anywhere but at this new school and took off running for home as soon as we were let out that afternoon. I couldn't run fast enough. Several of the boys—two first graders and a third grader—started chasing after me, so I ran all the harder. I burst into our apartment, gasping for breath, and told Mom that some kids were after me. She sent them away but, soon enough, I realized that my narrow escape had only made things worse. Days later, the same group of boys knocked on the front door after school.

"We want Wayne to come outside and fight," the third grader said to Mom. He wasn't asking.

She turned to me. "Douglas Wayne," she said matter-of-factly and out of their earshot, "If you don't go out there today, they'll never leave you alone. They'll be after you every day."

"I don't want to fight," I said.

She persisted. "I won't let them jump on you all at once," she said. "One at a time, you can fight them. You have to show you're not afraid."

Trembling, I walked outside. The three boys stared me in the face. They'd said okay to Mom's rules of engagement and, immediately, one of the first graders punched me in the face. I counterpunched to his stomach. He cried, and the first fight was over. A win. With my confidence boosted, I took on the next one. After exchanging a half dozen or so punches, we mutually agreed to call it a tie. That left the third grader, who was Bracy's size—a lot bigger than me. That fight was a loss, but I didn't get hurt seriously, and, having fought the older kid, I was left alone after that day. At six years old, I'd proven that I could and would fight if necessary.

Except in tussles with my brothers, I had never fought anyone before. I had never been cornered like that. I had never known boys like that, a pack of city kids, bullies, who'd just keep after you until you stood up to them. I discovered several important things that day. First, when it came to fighting, I had a natural talent; I was fast and my own strength surprised me. Second, I learned that I needed to take responsibility—to be prepared—to defend myself at any time against any threat or intimidation. I could no longer take my safety for granted. The boys' desire to fight me that day had been ignited by the belief that I feared them. Like honey is to bears, so is prey to predator. My fear had attracted them to me. Eventually, we became friends, but I learned a key lesson from that first fight: standing up to bullies significantly decreases the likelihood of becoming their victim.

That lesson was easier to apply at school than at home. It was in Granite City that I first began to notice unsavory things about my father and become afraid of him. He liked to drink. He had been drinking more and more, and he underwent a profound personality change when he was drunk. He began to be violent. For no obvious reason, he would seethe with irritation and his smoldering irritation would transform into uncontrollable rage, which nothing could appease. He began to abuse and beat my mother. I carry vivid memories of the words, images, and sickening sounds that accompanied these explosions. "I was drunk when I married you," he'd hurl at my mother, along with a barrage of profanities. Often I became physically ill standing by helplessly in our cramped quarters as my father hit and choked my mother. In my six-year-old mind, I believed that he was going to kill her. His violence triggered stark panic in me and in my brothers and sisters. Calming down under those circumstances, when it seemed Dad had lost complete control, was not possible. He would batter my mother with kicks, forceful blows of his fists, and by slamming her against the walls. If we tried to stop him, he would direct his violence against us with whatever was at hand—a switch, his belt, and his fists. When he was like that, he was capable of causing severe injuries to his entire family.

In addition to the stress of violence at home was the stress of insufficient food. Back in Stewart County, Papa Jim and Mamma Pearl and the other Wallaces had had our backs. Mom would let them know when we were out of groceries or couldn't pay the rent. But in Granite City, we were on our own. For days at a time, we sometimes lived on bread and gravy. Mom would have to brave a conversation with my father about the urgent need for food. He always got roaring mad. "What do you want me to do about it?" he would shout.

"Feed your children, Brady!" she would reply.

We never knew exactly what happened to my father's jobs in Granite City, only that little to no money was coming in.

Our first Christmas in Illinois, we had no food in the house. All of us were very hungry. It was Christmas Eve, frigid outside, and my father had been gone for days, it seemed. I remember my three-year-old brother, Steve, crying and pleading with Mom for something to eat. The hunger that would settle over us brought such sadness to our family. I think the sadness frightened me more than the lack of food. I assumed that everyone had hard times like we did. Mom could do nothing but pray. Please, God, save this family, she'd pray loudly. I thought she was shouting in case God wouldn't hear her otherwise.

In the morning came an unexpected knock on the door. Mom answered it to a trio of strangers bundled up against the cold.

"Merry Christmas!" one of the smiling women said. "We've come with presents and food for your family!"

"My prayers have been answered," said Mom with joy.

Our spartan, underfurnished living room was suddenly filled with excitement and the colors of Christmas wrapping and ribbons. In addition to the gifts, one for each of us, were turkey, ham, dressing, all sorts of vegetables, and desserts. We ate first and opened the presents after. The meal was sumptuous. Nothing since we'd come to Granite City could compare. My Christmas present was a toy car with speedy rubber wheels and metal hubcaps that I played with for most of the day. It rolled very fast and very far. I loved that car.

Later that night, Dad came home smelling of alcohol and wearing that familiar, vacant, glassy look in his eyes. He opened the refrigerator door and became enraged.

"Where did all this food come from?" he said, turning on Mom. "Have you found a boyfriend?"

"No. This was given to us in charity," she said.

Dad swung round and, with unleashed fury, hit her in the face with his fist, drawing blood. Instant panic seized the room. His punch had knocked my mother backward and to the ground, where she fought him off. Platters had been knocked off the kitchen table, grease and food strewn everywhere across the floor. I wanted to help Mom but, like my siblings, was frozen in a state of acute fear. My two sisters Faye and Donna were shrieking. I crouched into a corner by the back kitchen door, my eyes locked on Mom and Dad.

The incident stayed with me forever. I felt the urge to intervene, to protect my mother, but I did nothing. We tried to pretend that it had never happened—until it happened again. We tried to stay out of the house as much as possible whenever Dad was home. We played in the neighborhood park or rode the one bike we had. My older sister, Faye, and I usually rode the bike together. She sat on the handlebars and I did the pedaling, obligingly steering in any direction she wanted to go. At seven years old, Faye was afraid of strangers, particularly men, and often asked me to pedal faster whenever she sensed danger.

The misery index of our life in Granite City was high. For me, it was a dreadful place. A few months after Christmas we moved from the Kirkpatrick projects into an even smaller apartment above a drugstore on the corner of a very busy street. Our three rooms were tiny.

I remember my excitement at living over a corner store filled with candy in display shelves right below our bedroom. I couldn't wait to go inside. But the very first time, the white-haired lady proprietor grabbed me by the ear and proceeded to lecture me about the proper behavior of children who lived in the building. The grim-faced candy store owner, as it turned out, was also our landlady.

"We don't allow your kind in here," she said coldly.

"I just want to look at the candy," I said.

"Don't come in here again unless you have money in your pocket," she shot back. She looked at me as if I were a thief, although I'd never stolen anything, ever. She tugged at my ear again and led me out the front door to the street.

I felt ashamed and humiliated, a word not yet in my vocabulary. I felt as if I had done something wrong. For the first time, I felt the third-class status of being poor. As little as we'd had in Stewart County, I'd shared in the pride of the tight-knit, extended Wallace family, with Papa Jim its benevolent patriarch. The store owner had discarded me like so much trash. A stranger had turned my young world around, and pointed me toward the bottom.

CHAPTER THREE

Back to Tennessee

Eleven months after arriving in Granite City, we received news that Grandpa Ellis, my mother's father, had died of a heart attack while working his farm in Stewart County. From the fields, he had returned to the house pale and with chest pains. Grandma Mavis ran to the neighbors for help, leaving him sitting next to the fire. When she returned, Grandpa Ellis had collapsed near the wood-burning stove and his clothes had partially caught on fire. The fire was extinguished, but it was too late to save him. He had died.

Our first stop upon returning from Granite City was once again a temporary stay with Papa Jim and Mamma Pearl in their small two-bedroom farmhouse. My grandparents didn't have the resources to solve their son's myriad problems, financial or otherwise, but they were always willing to do what they could. I remember vividly my joy when Mom told us we were moving back to Stewart County, the immense relief. My grandparents' home was a shelter from the storm of the previous year's disquiet and violence, of my initiation to the dark side of human behavior. The trauma and stress of the past year had erased any measure of security and safety I might have had. Anxiety replaced inner calm. But at Papa Jim and Mamma Pearl's, I could feel the tension uncoil.

One evening I overheard Mamma Pearl complaining to my grandfather about his own drinking. She thought that Papa Jim and my father might be a bad influence on each other, drinking moonshine whiskey together as they did the chores around the farm. One day when they purchased their moonshine, I'd been allowed to come along. We drove for a while down an isolated dirt road before Papa Jim pulled over to the side and parked his car. From there, on foot, we followed a narrow, grassy path that led us to a steep hillside climb.

I followed along behind Papa Jim and Dad until we came to a large dilapidated shack, precariously situated on the flank of a towering rock formation. On the buckled front steps sat a wiry old man in overalls, his face deeply wrinkled, staring sideways in our direction. He and Papa Jim nodded in recognition to each other. They spoke briefly, out of my earshot. Papa Jim, Dad, and I then followed the old man along a little-worn trail that took us deep into the woods.

A pungent, sour odor greeted us as we approached a clearing in the forest. In the clearing stood several three-foot-high tin barrels positioned strategically over smoldering wood fires. It was dead quiet except for the crackling of the fires and the sound of nearby rushing water. The men took seats on a trio of tree stumps and began a low chatter. I stayed mobile. I walked over to inspect one of the cooking barrels, which was filled to the halfway point with corn kernels and water heated to a temperature below boiling. The corn was swollen and bleached to bright white from the aging and fermentation process. A swarm of flies circled the barrel, both inside and out. The odor was so rank that I had to back away.

Papa Jim and Dad bought two pint-size jars of the stuff. This was genuine moonshine, they told me. As Papa Jim drove us home around dusk, they took turns taking sips from one of the jars. That Papa Jim and Dad enjoyed each other's company immensely was obvious to me. Dad wore a broad smile and, in spite of everything, it pleased me to see him happy. I desperately wanted him to be happy.

Shortly after the moonshine incident our family moved from Papa Jim's home, and the cycle of moving every few weeks continued. Each house was primitive, falling down, without plumbing or electricity, and pretty much indistinguishable from the many others that had come before. We never had a telephone and, at night, our few coal-oil lamps flickered faint light into the front room. Otherwise, the bedrooms were pitch black.

For long periods our only income was the fifty-five-dollar government check that came without fail every month to Mom. That small check was the gift that kept on giving. Frugal by necessity, Mom knew how to stretch the fifty-five dollars to cover basic supplies. She would purchase lard, flour, and beans in bulk. The kitchen usually held a ten-pound bucket of lard. Biscuits and gravy were our staples.

Mom made all our soap—for washing clothes, the house, and us—although tackling the ever-present dirt in all those areas was mostly a losing proposition. To make the soap, Mom would rinse a heaping pile of wood ashes with water several times over until the ashes were reduced to a pasty, gray substance she called lye. Next, she would mix the lye with lard and then heat the mixture over the fire in the cast-iron kettle, stirring frequently with a broad paddle. Finally, the mixture would cool and harden, and she cut it into cakes about five inches long and a few inches thick. The unforgettable stench of lye soap permeated the air, both inside and outside the house.

In the dead heat of summer, the humidity seemed to hammer on the thin tin roofs. Day and night, we would leave the doors and windows open to allow for any stray breeze to come in. Moths, gnats, flies, and mosquitoes entered freely, causing great discomfort to all of us. At bedtime, I would pull the cover sheet over my head to keep away the army of insects. I couldn't understand how they managed to bite me anyway during the night in the most annoying places—behind the knee or in the small of my sweating back. The persistent drone became like the noise of a chainsaw in my ear.

The flies and mosquitoes, in particular, were a constant threat to our drinking water, which we captured from rainwater running off the roof. Gutters routed the rain down to a large metal barrel standing at a corner of the house. To prevent the flies and mosquitoes from laying their eggs, we kept the barrel covered in dry weather with a square iron plate. But in rainstorms, we would slide off the iron plate just long enough to freshen our cache.

By mid-June, we had removed both our shirts and our shoes and we kept them off all summer until the beginning of fall. Initially, we suffered blistering sunburns on our shoulders and legs, but both our legs and upper bodies soon darkened to deep brown.

Sometimes we lived near blacktop roads, which turned so soft under the sweltering summer sun that the macadam often boiled into blisters—about two inches round, like soap bubbles in a bath. This was endless amusement to me and my brothers, and we enjoyed the squishy feel of the black bubbles under our bare feet. Occasionally, one would burst and scorch the skin, but as soon as it healed, we'd return to the heat-bleared road. My mother used rags torn from old sheets to wrap our injuries, just as her mother had done for her when she was a child. By the end of the summer, our feet had usually become so tough that injuries were few.

Just as easily as summer could soar above one hundred degrees, winter could dip below freezing. Subzero temperatures were not unusual. I remember winter's bone-chilling cold seeping inside our exposed house. We had no insulation. Biting wind blew in through the roof, the cracks in the wood-planked walls, and the gaping holes in the floorboards. Traces of ice would accumulate on the outside of the house, as though begging to come in. On frigid nights, I would seize up with shivers as I slipped between freezing-cold sheets. I remember seeing the ghost of my breath as I lay in bed. My blood would try in vain to warm my body, especially since I had little to no body fat.

I shared a bed with my older brother Bracy and my younger brothers Steve and Rick. The bed consisted of an uneven, shallow mattress atop a wooden frame of wide, rough planks. My brothers and I would huddle close together under the covers until we were warm enough to relax and fall asleep. A lot of elbowing and pushing would go on during the night, but we were used to that kind of thing. It didn't interfere with our sleep. The preference was always for the inside in winter and the outside in summer.

In winter, the small living rooms were the only warm spots in the house and, even there, usually only right next to the pot-bellied stove. Mom would tack sheets over the windows and doorways—even the doorways to the bedrooms—to prevent heat loss.

Feeding its insatiable appetite for wood, we stoked the fire until the sides of the stove turned bright red.

My job was to tote the wood inside from the stack on the front porch and to pile it up behind the stove within easy grasp. The front door usually opened directly to the center of the living room, and my siblings often complained that I held the door open too long as I came and went, allowing in the icy cold air as they huddled together on our old, hand-me-down couch.

Even with the fire roaring, blankets and homemade quilts were necessary to keep warm. Most of our blankets came from my father's brother, Uncle Pete, who worked at the Fort Campbell military base nearby. Mamma Pearl and Grandma Mavis made the quilts from a patchwork of ripped shirts, frayed overalls, burlap sacks, or any other material that could be stitched together. If the patches tore, which they often did, we'd get a foot or leg twisted up in the quilt during the night. We would laugh when one of us tried getting out of bed in the morning all tangled up in a torn quilt. The family also got a laugh when, after bringing in an armload of firewood, I'd warm my backside against the stove and, on more than one occasion, back up too close and burn a half-dollar-size blister on my rear.

Once we were old enough to lift an axe, my brothers and I spent the majority of our time searching for firewood. Year-round, my mother needed firewood for cooking and heating water. Getting the wood wherever and whenever we could was the responsibility of my brothers and me, even if it meant not asking permission of the owner of the property upon which we were living. Firewood was critical for our survival. Living on the razor's edge, you tend to do things first and ask questions later.

While Bracy and I worked on the firewood and did the heavy lifting, like hauling water from the well, my older sister Faye helped Mom with the cleaning and cooking and with watching over the three younger ones—Steve, Donna, and Rick. We didn't have friends during those early years. We had our work and each other.

On our various expeditions, my brother and I frequently attracted stray dogs and dogs belonging to nearby farmhouses. They would hear us in the woods and bound over to where we were walking or working. We'd never had a dog, or any pet—a pet would be an extra mouth to feed—so we showered these dogs with love and affection, which only encouraged them to follow us home. Mom drew the line at dogs in the house. But one particular brindle-colored mutt had the dangerous habit of darting inside when the front door was accidentally left ajar. Mom warned us that if the dog entered the house again, she would douse him with boiling water from the stove. No way did I think that my sweet-natured mother could mean such a thing—until one day he did it again. Mom grabbed a cast-iron cooking pot and, true to her word, scalded the dog with boiling water. He yelped in pain and ran away at full speed. We listened to his cries until they could no longer be heard.

A few months after that incident, I became best friends with a black hunting dog—a stray—that I named Blackie. The backwoods were home to lots of adolescent dogs who'd been trained for coon hunting, surpassed by younger faster dogs, discarded, and then treated like coyotes by the locals.

With Blackie, the first thing I did was to train him not to follow me into the house and to stay outdoors at all times. Dad had largely been absent, but one day he came home from a drinking binge and saw me playing with Blackie in the yard. Like Mom, Dad didn't like strays lingering around the house, so he immediately instructed me to put the dog in his battered-up car.

Dad told me that he was going to take the dog back to his home, which I knew was unlikely. Alarmed, I leapt into the backseat with Blackie. We drove for a dozen miles, which on bumpy back roads can seem like twenty. Then, halfway across the Cumberland River Bridge, Dad stopped the car, opened the back door, grabbed Blackie from my arms, and threw him off the bridge into the deep river forty feet below. I jumped out of the car and watched in horror as Blackie struggled for traction in midair and then plunged into the fast-moving, cold water of the Cumberland River.

My father grabbed my arm. "Get back into the car," he said.

Three days later, Blackie showed up on the front porch, looking fragile and exhausted, but otherwise okay. My father, who just happened to be home, spotted him right away. In a flash, he shoved Blackie in the trunk of his car and drove him away again. This time Blackie didn't come back. After that, I made sure to discourage any dogs from hanging around the house. I continued making friends with dogs but trained them to follow me only as far as the front yard. My home was not a safe place for dogs.

CHAPTER FOUR

Poverty Keeps You Hungry

When Dad was not working, usually Bracy and I also spent a lot of our time helping to feed the family. We worked in the vegetable garden and hammered taps into the trunks of maple trees, setting galvanized buckets underneath to catch the sap. Mom used the maple sap for syrup and also as sugar for breads and pies. For a family surviving mainly on biscuits, beans, and gravy, the addition of sugar was ambrosia.

Bracy hunted for game in the woods—our family was always hungry for meat—while I fished the local creeks. I became an experienced fisherman by the age of seven. I used a long, thin, freshly cut cane pole, an assortment of hooks and sinkers, homemade bobbers, and freshly caught bait. Sometimes, the sinkers were nothing more than nuts, bolts, or spark plugs. I'd pack up my gear and take a good long walk to a fishing spot—traveling solo unless my younger brother, Steve, came along. As I made my way upstream, I would catch fresh crawfish for bait from beneath the rocks in the shallow creek beds.

Usually, it took a couple of hours to catch enough for a good day's fishing. If Steve were with me, he'd lift the rocks while I snatched the quick-darting crawfish with my hands. Occasionally, we swept up some small frogs too, which also made excellent bait.

At the fishing spot—I had favorites by midsummer—we strung a single fishing line across the creek by tying the line to trees on opposite sides of the creek. From the cross-line, we suspended four other fishing lines, each one baited with a different lure, and then we'd take a spot on the grassy bank to cane-pole fish, suffering the aggravation of chigger bites on our legs, arms, and backs. At the end of the day, we would put fresh bait on each of the four dangling lines and leave them for night fishing. Usually, we returned home with a nice string-load of catfish, which Mom immediately gutted, cleaned, and then fried up for supper.

By the age of ten, Bracy was a tenacious and patient squirrel hunter who knew the secrets of stalking his prey. He preferred to hunt immediately after a shower or rainstorm when the leaves on the forest floor are wet and make no noise when stepped on by a hunter. A squirrel would disappear at the faintest rustle of a single leaf. As soon as the rain stopped, Bracy would quickly grab his twenty-two single-shot rifle, a gift from our mother's younger brother, Uncle Virgil, and head out the door.

A squirrel, to camouflage his body, will hug a tree, pressing itself flat against the trunk and remaining very still. You can scan the entire trunk of a tree and miss a squirrel completely even though it's right before your eyes. If a squirrel detects that it's been spotted, in a flash it will dart to the opposite side of the tree. You can circle the tree all day long and never see the squirrel. On days that I accompanied him, Bracy would direct me to shake a branch on one side of the tree to cause the squirrel to dash to the opposite side, where Bracy was poised to shoot. Using a single-shot rifle meant that he only had one bullet to get his prey, so the aim had to be accurate.

Bracy hunted for rabbits too. He walked the fields for hours hoping to spook a rabbit from its hiding place in the brush. Whenever he spotted one, usually tearing across the open field, he gave a loud, high-pitched whistle. The rabbit would stop dead in its tracks and perk up its ears. That's when Bracy took the opportunity to shoot.

He brought home fresh meat often that summer.

Mom fried up the rabbits and squirrels with lard and made a gravy and meat mixture that we poured over biscuits for a delicious meal. She even used the brains of the squirrel to mix with gravy for breakfast.

To feed our family of eight—seven, if Dad was absent—Mom had to be ingenious in supplementing our harvest of garden vegetables. She taught us how to identify edible native plants. Nearly every day we set out to the fields and forests in search of food—nuts from hickory and walnut trees, occasional wild apples, and the leaves, twigs, and root bark of the small sassafras tree that made tea, flavored soups and, when chewed, freshened your breath. You could even use the tender, shredded sassafras twigs to brush your teeth with.

In the open fields we checked for wild green onions and a wild lettuce-like plant called thistleweed. Mom often made our green salads with this weedy plant of thin, green leaves tapering to a sharp point. Her salad dressing was a mixture of lard and native herbs. As summer grew hotter, the thistleweed acquired a slightly bitter taste but was still edible. We also checked the fence rows for poke—short for *pokeweed*—another wild, weedy plant with large leaves similar to turnip greens, only a darker green. Picking a mess of it always created sticky green stains on our hands and clothes. Mom would boil it, like collard greens, to make what folks in Stewart County called "poke salad." Poke salad often served as our primary vegetable. Like thistleweed, its taste was bitter, more or less, depending on the summer heat.

On the hillsides, wild blackberries were plentiful. We'd go in search of them for desserts that Mom would try to make for us in summer. Enough berries for a family of our size meant two to four hours of steady picking. Because blackberry bushes tend to grow in bunches hidden amid thickets of thorns, by the end of the day, our hands and arms were pricked, scratched, and full of cuts. Back home, we had to carefully remove every thorn splinter that had become embedded in our skin, and there could be many. Undetected thorn pricks easily became infected, although Mom had a treatment. She would wrap the inflammation with a bandage of fatback bacon provided by Papa Jim. We'd wear the bandage overnight and by morning, the bacon would have drawn both the infection and the thorn splinter from our skin. Once the thorn was gone, the sore would heal up quickly.

In July 1957, shortly after my eighth birthday, Mom had another idea that she'd gotten from a magazine advertisement—two hundred baby chickens, delivered right to your door, for only fifteen dollars. Mom made the decision to do it, using fifteen dollars of her fifty-five-dollar monthly check. The chickens would bring an abundance of both meat and eggs, she thought.

A few weeks later, two hundred, two-day-old, fluffy baby chicks arrived in a ventilated cardboard box. Without any forethought, we released them into the yard and, immediately, they scattered in all directions, chirping and flapping their fluffy yellow wings. Only then did the magnitude of their arrival hit Mom and the rest of us with full force. We had neither food nor shelter for the chicks. The first night, they huddled underneath the cracked floorboards of the house, all two hundred of them chirping all night long. During the day, they foraged frantically hither and yon for food. Within forty-eight hours, it became apparent that Mom had made a colossal mistake.

In short order, the chicks not only had the run of the yard but, at times, also the house. If the front door was left open accidentally, in they would come. During dinner, if you tried to shoo them out, they'd leap and scurry across the table. They'd run across your plate. Outside, their droppings were scattered throughout the front and back yards. You couldn't walk to or from the house without stepping in the droppings. As they grew older and even wilder, the chickens were impossible to catch. We never had a single one for a meal.

As summer waned, the chickens began disappearing. Some died for unknown reasons. Evidence of predators appeared. Some simply vanished into the woods. The interminable noise slowly came to an end, but was replaced by an intolerable odor from within the house. Mom began pulling away the plaster from the walls and, inside, she found dead baby chickens piled several feet deep. For the next few days, all of us worked tearing out the interior walls and scrubbing the house thoroughly, top to bottom. It took a while for the smell in the house to return to normal. That was Mom's one and only entrepreneurial adventure.

CHAPTER FIVE

"I'm Going to Be a Lawyer"

E ach year from September through June, Mom made sure we went to school as soon as we were old enough, even if we were dressed in rags. Stewart County was home to about seven one-room schoolhouses and, in the fall of 1957, Bracy, Faye, and I were enrolled in one of them, the New Haven School on old Highway 79, which connected Dover and Clarksville, the closest towns of any size. Established in 1889, the small, paint-worn, clapboard school consisted of a wood-planked porch; a cloak area; a pot-bellied stove in a large, open classroom; and a teacher.

I was enrolled in third grade, Faye in fourth, and Bracy in fifth.

We sat at wooden desks—we each had our own—in eight rows according to grade level. In the first row sat the first graders, in the back row the eighth graders. About thirty kids attended the school that year, the majority of them in the earlier grades. I remember this school because I had my first crush ever, on Evelyn Hicks, who was in second grade and thus sat in the row in front of me.

At the ringing of the morning bell, the teacher took attendance and then, beginning with the first grade, moved from row to row teaching each class its specific lesson for the day. When not working directly with the teacher, we were required to read or write, and so went the school day. Being in one room forced us all to work together. Older students helped the younger ones with their studies. And the younger ones readily soaked up the experience of the sixth, seventh, and eighth graders. Camaraderie existed among the different ages. The teacher was kind. I felt safe. I liked that school.

After two months, though, we moved again, about five miles away, to Big Rock, one of the few places we lived that you could sometimes find on a map. The town consisted of a country store and a post office. That was it. A giant limestone rock—nine stories high and just as wide—had given the town its name.

We arrived in Big Rock around Thanksgiving, moving into the biggest house our family had ever lived in—or ever would again. The house had two stories, four bedrooms, upper and lower porches, and lots of windows. It wore the look of a once-upon-a-time grand home that had long since been neglected. The porches drooped, the paint had peeled down to the wood, the windowsills had rotted, and a thousand cracks let cold air blow through. But for a young boy who had only lived in small rundown places, this large rundown place seemed nice. I had never been inside a house with two levels before. It didn't have running water or indoor plumbing, but it had electricity. And somehow we managed to move in with enough money to have the electricity turned on.

Big Rock's elementary school was a two-room schoolhouse, with a gym, lunchroom, fully equipped playground, and two teachers, one of whom was the principal. Although it was a small country school, Big Rock shared a few social similarities to the school we had attended in Granite City. On my first day, the bullies started circling. So I applied the lesson I'd learned in first grade. I stood up to them and fought. Many of the bullies had older brothers at Big Rock and, often, having won a fight against one brother, I'd have to fight the other. Bracy was in the same situation and had to fight almost every day at school. We both paid with black eyes and bloody noses. One time, after I beat his younger brother in a fight, a kid and his friends ambushed me on the playground, slamming my face into a metal pole and chipping my right front tooth. To this day, that tooth is still chipped.

Big Rock echoed Granite City in another way as well. The ill-tempered lady proprietor in Illinois had ejected me from her store because I was poor, and my family was poor. Her caustic disrespect had been my first personal taste of discrimination at six years old. At Big Rock School, at eight years old, I got my second taste.

I couldn't help but notice that kids who wore nice clean clothes to school were popular. These were the same kids who talked about summer vacations, birthday parties, and county fairs—experiences foreign to me. My school outfit consisted of a pair of pants, a shirt, a wool jacket, a pair of shoes, and a single pair of white socks. I owned no sweater, underwear, hat, or gloves. As soon as I got home from school, I exchanged my school clothes for my work clothes. None-theless, by the end of the school year, my school clothes were stained and ragged.

The school provided a warm lunch to all students for a charge of twenty-five cents—more than my family could afford. So, to pay for my lunch, I was required to work for an hour a day during class breaks. Bracy and Faye had to work as well. We mopped hallways, swept floors, assisted in the lunchroom and, in warmer weather, cleaned up outside as well. Sometimes, if help was needed right away, we'd be taken out of the classroom. The three of us talked to each other about the embarrassment. I deeply resented forfeiting my school breaks and being set apart from my classmates. It didn't help that my classmates teased me about being a day laborer. When you work for your lunch at school and you dress in the same set of soil-stained clothes, day after day, you're treated differently.

Quite quickly, I realized that Bracy, Faye, and I were the poorest students at the school. There wasn't a lot of money floating around Stewart County. But on a relative scale, we were at the bottom. There was nowhere for me to hide—especially from my own awareness of my circumstances. Other than my brother and sister, I didn't feel close to anyone at this school.

I actively began to dream of the day when I would no longer be poor. I spent hours fantasizing about the kind of profession I would choose. I didn't know any lawyers at the time, but for some reason that's where my imagination took me, that was the career that grabbed hold of me. Plus I'd heard somewhere that lawyers make a lot of money. I wanted to make my fortune. So, in the third grade, I decided to become an attorney. I was certain I could become one of the most successful lawyers that Stewart County had ever known.

One day, Big Rock's principal came to my classroom. He asked each of us what we wanted to be when we grew up. When he directed the question to me, I said proudly and without hesitation, "I am going to be a lawyer!" A ripple of laughter and whispering spread throughout the classroom.

Later on, one of students who hadn't been laughing explained it to me.

"You're poor, Wayne," he told me. "You can't afford college. You have to go to college to become a lawyer. College is too expensive for families like yours."

I had already assumed that the laughter and whispering was because of the incongruity of a poor boy like me giving voice to such an outsized ambition, and that stung. But what came as a surprise was that there were limitations on that ambition. Ridicule was one thing; that the door might be shut to me was another. Having lived a relatively isolated life in which I'd been allowed to roam wild and free a good deal of the time, I didn't fully grasp that poverty imposed such obstacles. I was finding out.

I asked my teacher for permission to see the principal—after all, it was he who'd raised the question. We met in his small office. Fortyish and balding, in a white short-sleeved shirt and tie, the principal sat behind his desk and I sat across from him in an uncomfortable wooden chair. I could see the playground out the window behind him.

"Take a seat, son," he'd said.

He was a stern man, but I'd known sterner. I wasn't afraid of him; I wanted an explanation.

Looking back on it now, I realize that of course he knew all about my family—the Black Wallaces and my father's reputation as the local drunk. No doubt he also knew of my frequent fighting. He probably thought I was wasting his time.

He listened. He appeared sympathetic but, finally, discouraging.

College and law school were unlikely options for me, he said. Establish realistic goals, he advised, goals based upon the reality of my family's resources. He recommended that I consider a career in farming. There were some very successful farmers in Stewart County, he assured me.

"I can own a farm *and* be a successful lawyer," I said.

He seemed irritated. "You'll learn soon enough," he said, sighing and bringing the conversation to an end.

Like acid on copper, the whole episode etched itself in my memory. I knew then that if I were to have a life, if I were to look beyond my circumstances, I would have to make it happen on my own.

CHAPTER SIX

Don't Kill That Mockingbird

W e lasted until spring in the two-story house before we had to leave. We moved around like nomads. One house was pretty much the same as another, and it was hard to keep track. But one thing I remember about the next place was that it was only a few miles away and still fell within the Big Rock school district, and it had an electric stove for cooking and a refrigerator. That was good news. It meant less firewood was needed, which gave us leisure time to enjoy the beautiful Tennessee landscape.

Bracy, Steve, and I would take off at dawn on weekends and spend the entire day out-of-doors. In hill country—the landscape we were born into—spring is the sweet spot between the extremes of winter and the logy heat of summer. The greenery and wildflowers explode. The air is sweet. The rushing creeks practically sing.

The forest floor offered a year-round supply of leaves. During cool mornings, we'd run down the hills and "monkey-trot"—our version of pole-vaulting—which catapulted us high into the air and hurled us as much as twenty feet into a soft, thick layer of leaves. We would do this over and over, monkey-trotting down one hill after another, until the game switched to swinging vines.

We were always on the lookout for the tangled native vines that hung from the tallest trees in the woods. These strong vine ropes supported our weight and were thrilling to ride, allowing us to swing out far and wide. We would grab tight hold of a vine, make a fast running start, and lunge ourselves off the steep bank of a creek, sometimes swinging back, sometimes letting go and dropping to the water below if we deemed it deep enough. The creek water was always teeth-chattering cold. All three of us would swing from the vines for hours, creating paths with our feet as we glided up and back.

When we got thirsty, we drank liberally from the pure fresh water of the creeks, which we explored endlessly. The creeks could be ankle-deep in some spots and then, a hundred yards down, become a six-foot-deep swimming hole. Walking the creek beds, you never knew what would lie around the bend. A creek might narrow into a deep gully or open out to a beaver dam deep with fish or suddenly merge with another creek into rushing, white water.

Blooming dogwoods often lined the creek beds. From the Y-shaped forks of their branches, we discovered how to make our own slingshots—we called them "flip-forks." For the elastic band, we'd hunt for old tires—abandoned cars were plentiful in Stewart County—and cut thin, one-inch strips of rubber from the inner tubes. We used the tongues of discarded shoes for the pouch. We then stitched it all together using twine, the hardest of our materials to find. Our usual method was to ask a neighboring farmer for some and, if he said no, to keep on asking until somebody said yes. We were always on the lookout for twine.

I came up with the idea of using our flip-forks for hunting. Our first outings were rough but, on one particular day, much to my surprise, I managed to get close enough to a Canadian goose to succeed and, with a broad smile, delivered the fat goose to Mom. Straightaway, she plucked, butchered, cleaned, and cooked the bird for dinner. All of us were salivating at the thought of tasting our first goose meat. However, it took only a few bites to realize the meat was far too tough to eat. It tasted and chewed like shoe leather, and everyone sitting at the table seemed to have come to this realization at the same time. From the pained look on everyone's face, it was clear that we were in agreement. We had a big laugh over our struggle to swallow the old bird and fed the goose to some delighted stray dogs.

One day, getting on summer, I was out on my own and aiming my flip-fork at a gray, robin-size bird perched on a fence rail in an open pasture about a quarter-mile from home.

"Don't kill that mockingbird," I heard someone say from behind.

The man's voice belonged to a man named Philip, who lived about a quarter-mile down the road. You couldn't see his house from ours, but he was our closest next-door neighbor. He spoke with a northern accent.

"Why not?" I said, puzzled.

"That's a mockingbird," he answered. "The Tennessee state bird."

"How do you know it's a mockingbird?" I said.

"See the long, fan-shaped tail feathers? Listen to her sing. Why would you want to kill such a beautiful thing?"

I had no answer.

"How about those birds over there?" he said, pointing to a pair of tiny birds with black heads and white throats sitting together on a bush about ten feet away. Only three or four inches long, these birds looked like little fluffballs. "Do you want to kill them too?"

"Maybe," I said uncertainly.

"Those are black-capped chickadees. Mates. They probably have a nest of babies somewhere close. Do you plan to kill the whole family?"

I felt a sickly feeling in my stomach. I had never thought of birds being part of a family.

"I wouldn't do that," I said.

Thus began my education about birds. Philip took me under his wing. I had never known anyone who cared so much about animals. More than that, no one had ever taken an interest in educating me about anything outside the school curriculum. He was a good and patient teacher, who talked about birds as if they were family members. He was willing to spend as much time teaching me as I could give him, even though he had a job, a wife, and a baby boy younger than two years of age. He showed me his many books on birds and took me on bird-watching hikes, which would last for an hour or two. He taught me to watch for flying patterns and to listen to the sounds—their mating calls, their cries of distress, their songs of happiness.

In the beginning, it took a few weeks just to understand the concept of studying birds, but one day I got it. I learned that birds have personalities and families, some are beautiful though others are not, and all face constant danger and are forever in search of food. I could understand that. I learned how to identify birds by their appearances, colors, and unique sounds. The more I learned about birds, the less interested I became in hunting them. I went from being a bird hunter to a bird-watcher.

I became particularly interested in a bird known locally as the rain crow—the yellow-billed cuckoo. Folks in Stewart County believed that this bird's call—a rapid, staccato *kuk-kuk-kuk-ceaow-ceaow-ceaow*—meant that rain was coming. The rain crow is a slender, olive-brown bird with a bright white belly and large white spots on the ends of its long, black, outer tail feathers. The females lay their eggs in nests built in thickets low to the ground. If someone approaches the nest, to protect her eggs or babies, the female will throw herself to the ground feigning injury, fluttering and tumbling and uttering loud, guttural calls of distress until the intruder backs away.

One day while I was walking in the woods, a rain crow suddenly darted toward me and dropped to the ground. By that time, I had learned about the female's protective style. I walked on, but on the way back the same rain crow startled me and again tumbled to the ground. I knew her nest must be close by. After some searching, underlying a low-lying bush, I found a frail twig-nest, perfectly camouflaged, and holding four smooth, light blue-green eggs.

A few days later, I returned to find four wild baby birds in the nest. As newly hatched chicks, they were ugly and scrawny and sported thorny-looking quills. Excited, I became a regular visitor. Within a few days, the babies were hopping freely within the bush, from tiny branch to tiny branch. I badly wanted one as a pet, which proved difficult. They were getting ready to fledge when, after many false starts, I finally managed to palm one of the tiny birds with my hands. The chick pecked at my fingers furiously.

I named him Willie and, at first, kept him inside a cage that I fashioned from a milk crate and a piece of old screen. Studiedly, I fed him caterpillars and other insects. His wings would vibrate rapidly when he wanted more. Once he'd had enough, he would trill a sound of satisfaction—*kuk-currrr*. Quickly, he became my friend and companion. Perching on a low branch in the front yard was his favorite spot. He also liked to sit on my shoulder when I hiked the hills. Sometimes he would fly ahead and I would follow after him by the sound of his calls. He was keenly affectionate and nestled himself in the crook of my neck, where he would twitch his wings in such a ticklish way that I could barely stand it. He'd peck gently behind my ears and in my hair, like he was preening me. But after a few weeks, Willie grew fearful of other humans, of my brothers and sisters. Then one day, he flew away and never came back. I mourned the loss for a long time.

CHAPTER SEVEN

Stoning Father

One midsummer afternoon in 1958, Dad stomped into the house with that familiar filmy, dull look in his eyes. I felt my heart contract. I told myself to stay calm. He started harassing Mom, blaming her for everything wrong in his life. He lunged for her and knocked her backward. Slipping out of his grasp, Mom gathered the kids, and swiftly ushered us outside the house. Dad tore after us out the front door, but then stopped abruptly on the edge of the front porch, as though he'd had a better idea, and leaned against the post. Blue-jeaned, gangly, and unshaven, he just stood there, staring at us with vacant eyes as the six of us kids stared back at him from the road where we were huddled around Mom. Dad began to snarl threats at Mom, warning her to come back into the house at once or else. Mom stood absolutely still, holding the hands of the two littlest ones, Ricky and Donna. She glanced back and forth between him and us. We were waiting for a signal from her to run.

"I'm not coming back into that house, Brady," she said. "You leave us alone." My heartbeat quickened.

She turned to us and pointed to the gravel on the road. "Hurry now, pick up those rocks, and make a big pile—right here by me."

Bracy, Faye, Steve, and I flew into motion gathering up the largest gravel rocks we could find and tossing them as fast as we could into a heap in front of Mom. I was trembling with adrenaline. Suddenly, my father leapt off the porch and came running toward us fast. His scowling face looked distorted. Then Mom bent down, picked up a handful of rocks, and threw them at him hard. Mom's arms were very strong.

"Help me!" she commanded us.

So I picked up a rock and threw it at Dad, still charging. My brothers and sister followed suit. A volley of rocks thundered down on Dad until he turned around and darted back to the safety of the porch.

"I'll get you for this," he said under his breath, then slammed the door behind him in outrage.

Mom led us up the road a good distance, where we hid for hours in a copse of small cedar trees. We barely talked, and when we did, it was in whispers. All was silent from the house except, a few times, Dad stepped out onto the porch and yelled more threats.

When it grew dark, Mom crept up to the front window and peered in to see if Dad had fallen asleep. She returned to the bushes and told us it was still dangerous, which meant only one thing—he was still awake and drinking. We were exhausted, hungry, and also underdressed for the cool night air. Mom snuck back to the house again and quietly walked around to the back porch and retrieved an old rollaway bed. My brothers and I dragged it about a hundred yards away from the house into a neighboring tobacco field.

Somehow, we all managed to fall asleep on that single rollaway bed that night, our body heat keeping each other warm. The next morning at dawn, we were awakened by the tobacco farmer in a hat and overalls, who must have been startled to see the seven of us sleeping in the middle of his field. All of us were mute except for Mom, who did the talking and didn't mince words about why we were there.

Without delay, the farmer took off for our house. We watched Dad answer the door and our neighbor, clearly not afraid of Dad, shake his finger in Dad's face. And so we went home. The farmer told us that he'd informed Dad that he had a nice family and that he should be ashamed of himself for what he had done. He warned Dad not to retaliate against any of the children for throwing rocks—a suggestion given to our neighbor by my mother. Dad must have agreed because the episode was dropped.

A month later, near the end of summer, Dad asked me early one morning if I wanted to go fishing with him. His clear eyes told me he was sober. I had never gone fishing with my father before. Thrilled, I began making preparations. I gathered up my fishing gear—my cane pole, string of fishing twine, assorted fishing hooks, and a supply of lead weights for bottom fishing.

"You won't need all that," Dad said. He told me that we were going to go fishing *his* way. He seemed excited about that, so I became excited too. We drove a ways in Dad's car until we came to a road that was really no more than a grassy path across open pastureland. I knew this path well. I had walked it many times. It led to one of my favorite fishing holes.

What happened next happened quickly. Dad parked his car, raised the hood, removed the battery, and set it on the creek bank. He told me that we were going to catch more fish than I had ever seen in my life. From his fishing bag, I watched him take three sticks of dynamite, each about eight inches long and an inch in diameter, and some long wire. He banded the dynamite together, connected the wires, and told me to get behind a tree. I'd become terribly ill at ease. He then threw the dynamite into the deepest part of the creek. He touched the ends of the wires to the posts of the car battery and, instantaneously, the creek exploded. The deafening noise of it shot through my body. The spray of water was enormous. Four or five dead fish lay at my feet. I felt unable to take in what had just happened.

Dad wore a half-smile. "Hurry up," he said. "Get the fish before they float away!" He was pointing toward the center of the creek. Scores of fish, big and small, had floated to the surface. "Move it, Wayne. We don't have all day!"

As ordered, I got down into the creek and picked up as many fish as I could, throwing them onto the bank, many slipping out of my fingers. A few catfish were in the mix and their sharp fin bones cut my hands. Repelled by what I had to do, I could feel tears lurking behind my eyes. I tripped my way downstream to get to the fish being carried away by the current as hundreds of tiny dead minnows sailed by me. Dad was acting jumpy, nervous, furtive, yelling at me to speed it up. *Dynamiting fish is probably illegal*, I thought to myself. I knew it was wrong. Dad seemed to be missing some source of kindness. He did catch more fish that day than I'd ever seen in my life, as he'd promised. But I felt ashamed.

CHAPTER EIGHT

The Gift of Giving

The beginning of fourth grade at Big Rock School felt promising. From the year before, I knew the terrain. I wasn't a stranger. On the first day, some of us were sent to see a nurse and a dentist at a temporary clinic set up in the school gymnasium. This is my first memory of ever having seen a medical professional or a dentist. The nurse gave me immunizations and the dentist spent two days filling my multiple cavities. Bracy, Faye, Steve, and I were probably the only students at Big Rock grateful to have a dentist working on our teeth. Steve had just started first grade.

One day that fall, Dad and Papa Jim drove to Dover one Saturday afternoon and took me with them. The two-lane road snaked through heavy woods that were beautiful, flaming with color. Dover was the county seat, eight miles away, with a population of a little over a thousand. It didn't offer a movie theater, but it had a gas station, a two-story red-brick courthouse, a jail, a town square, and more shopping options than anywhere else in Stewart County. As instructed, I was waiting in the busy town square for Dad and Papa Jim to finish their errands when I heard a woman call out to me, "Are you one of Brady Wallace's boys?"

I turned to see a woman of Mamma Pearl's age sitting in the back-seat of a black 1940s sedan and wearing a black, wide-brimmed hat. Her smile was warm. She seemed to know me.

"Yes, ma'am," I said.

"Well, then," she said, stepping out of her car. "Come right on over here and let me take a closer look at you."

She held her arms open and embraced me strongly, pressing her cheek against mine. I had no idea who she was or what she might want of me. Looking directly into my eyes, she said, "Do you know who I am?"

I thought she might be a distant relative, but I didn't recognize her.

"No, ma'am."

"Your name is Douglas Wayne Wallace, isn't it?" More a state-ment of fact than a question.

I nodded.

"Bless you, child. I'm Miss Dony. Let me tell you how it is that I know you."

Uncomprehending, I listened as Miss Dony told me that, nine years before, she had been present as the midwife to my mother and me when I was born—a most startling and intimate disclosure. She told me that, earlier that summer day, she'd had a premonition that something was about to happen that would require her assistance. The feeling was so strong she'd been compelled to cancel plans to visit a relative. She was sitting in a rocking chair on her front porch, waiting, when my two-and-a-half-year-old brother Bracy came run-ning for help up the road.

As she told me the story, I felt an immediate and unexpected close-ness to her, of the forever variety. Her great kindness seemed an impossible thing to me, and, yet, here she was right in front of me, letting some light into my world.

When she finished talking, she took a fifty-cent piece out of her purse and put it in my hand.

"This is for you," she said.

It was more money that I had ever had at any one time in my life.

I thanked her and then ran into a drugstore located just off the square. In a glass case, I spotted a necklace with a silver chain.

"How much for that necklace?" I asked the man behind the counter.

"Fifty cents."

I bought the necklace and ran back to Miss Dony's car as it was starting to pull away. I waved for it to stop.

"What's wrong, child?" she asked.

"This is for you," I said. I placed the necklace in her hand. I'll never forget her lovely smile.

CHAPTER NINE

Baloney

In mid-November, Dad came home one day with a ten-pound stick of fresh baloney. The look and the smell of it were powerful. We were often in a state of hunger, but especially for meat, which we had so rarely in our home. And baloney was the meat that all of us loved the most.

Dad put the baloney front and center on the kitchen table and then stepped outside to walk the hundred and fifty feet to the outhouse. The moment he was out of sight, we pounced on the baloney like a pack of coyotes and ate the sausage in its entirety. When he came back and saw what we'd done, he glowered, fists clenched. We realized we had made a serious mistake—the sight of the baloney had eclipsed any awareness that Dad had been drinking.

Dad was the central figure in our home but, because of his drinking, we lived in constant fear of him and were happiest when he wasn't around. He had a preference for drinking his moonshine and beer in bars or other places away from home. After being gone on a binge for days, or even a week sometimes, he'd return home to recover. After recovering, he'd go out and repeat the whole cycle—with the odd job thrown in between. His arrival home might occur at any hour of the day or night. We had to be on the alert and ready to run at a moment's notice.

Dad's heart turned coal black when he was drunk. And he seemed blind to the destruction he was creating. The day we ate the baloney, predictably, Dad erupted and came after us all. Mom stepped in front and he struck her. Before I knew what I was doing, I grabbed a heavy jar of pickles off the table and slammed it against the back of my father's head. The blow dazed and disoriented him enough that we scattered and, once again, spent a good part of the night outside—a November night this time. Later, once he'd passed out, we slipped back into the house and slept with Mom behind our locked bedroom door.

I had never struck my father, never confronted him in such a personal and violent way before. When he came to, I didn't know what he might do to me. I slept restlessly, afraid that he would break down the door and attack me while I was sleeping.

The next morning, I got up at first light and left the house. I needed time to think. I walked and walked. I was worried enough to be an old man. I worried for my own safety. I worried that I was trapped in a spiral of violence that was destined to repeat itself over and over again. How my father reacted to this particular incident, I figured, didn't really matter, because nothing was ever going to change. My father would hit Mom again, and I would be forced to come to her defense again. I worried that I would never have a normal relationship with my father. Deep in the woods, I cried and cried at the loss of that possibility.

Many hours later, I walked back to the house. Mom came outside to reassure me that Dad would not retaliate against me. I walked back inside. I wasn't shaking. He was sitting at the kitchen table.

"Come over here, Wayne, and sit down." He motioned for me to take the seat next to him.

"Yes, sir," I said, taking the seat opposite him to keep open my running options.

I raised my head and looked him in the eyes. I didn't see any anger. He seemed to be studying me, like he was trying to figure me out.

"I'm not going to punish you, son," he said, after a while. "I was drunk and acted badly."

He then pointed out that I had *also* acted badly by hitting him. A flash of hair-trigger anger passed over his face.

"You better not ever do that again," he said, staring straight into my eyes.

I was silent.

"Do you understand me, Wayne?"

"Yes, sir."

CHAPTER TEN

Coming Home an Angry Man

L ife continued on in the same pattern; year after year our family struggled to survive, moving from house to house, and relying upon relatives for necessities. Dad's drunken behavior in particular continued to plague the family, but I soon learned that my father was not the tough man he acted at home. The summer I turned twelve Dad offered to teach me how to drive. More than anything I wanted to learn how to drive a car. I was thrilled when he made the offer. Dad changed cars about as often as he changed houses, but I can remember this one—a crumpled 1954 Ford sedan, its blue paint worn clear to the metal in places.

To my surprise, I had it down on the first day. Dad taught me how to steer, to shift gears, to brake on the loose gravel roads—of which there were plenty in Stewart County.

That summer I spent a lot of time behind the wheel of Dad's car. On some days, he let me drive solo. One August morning, a few weeks before school started back up, Dad asked me if I wanted to drive the car while he ran some errands. Excited, I accepted immediately. Directed by Dad, I made the first two stops picking up two of his drinking buddies. He told them that I was in driver-training and would be the chauffeur for the day. His confidence in my newly acquired driving ability filled me with pride.

All morning, I drove my father and his friends around the county. The three of them drank beer, talked trash, and laughed it up. From time to time, sitting next to me in the front passenger seat, Dad would instruct me to take a turn here or a turn there. Mostly, he kept his focus on his friends. The three of them got drunker and drunker, and the car reeked of alcohol. One of Dad's friends asked me to pull the car over to the side of the road so he could be sick.

Around noon, near Dover, we stopped at a small country store where the men bought more beer, thick slices of baloney, saltine crackers, hot sauce, and an RC Cola for me. I loved baloney and saltine cracker sandwiches.

We took the food to yet another guy's place who had an old picnic table set down in the trees near a swift-flowing creek. The guy didn't seem to be expecting us, but neither did he seem surprised. We all sat down to lunch. I overheard Dad asking this man if he had any moonshine—moonshine was always preferable to beer—and realized we were at the home of a bootlegger. The bootlegger suggested we switch vehicles and head to a different creek nearby. He pitched the keys to his own car to me and said, "You drive, son."

The car was a shiny, four-door, scarlet-red Oldsmobile loaded down with chrome. I was so excited I was shaking. The bootlegger pointed me across a wide, grassy pasture to a nearly invisible tire path running parallel to the creek. The tire tracks were hidden by dark green fescue grass that stood taller than the car hood. Driving through it was a strange sensation, the high grass rubbing against the bottom of the car. I worried about getting us stuck in mud or a sinkhole. *Just keep the wheels on the tracks*, I told myself. Eventually, the path opened out to a secluded hilltop clearing, with a stand of oaks and a stunning view of a sun-dappled, rushing creek below. Well hidden, the spot was flanked on three sides by a large rock quarry, a low-lying marsh, and the creek. The grass-camouflaged tire path was the only way in or out.

I stayed with the car while Dad and the other men took a walk into the woods toward the quarry. The air all around was redolent of moonshine whiskey. A short while later, they returned with several full pint-size jars and spent the rest of the afternoon drinking. On my own, I took off on foot and explored the creek beds in both directions. By the time I got back to the clearing, the men were playing craps on the ground. All four doors to the red Oldsmobile stood open and the radio was blasting "Your Cheatin' Heart." The four men were huddled in a circle, throwing dice, and betting money with every throw, dollar bills piled high in the center. I was watching, trying to figure out how the game was played, when Dad handed me the dice and told me to roll for him. With the slurring and swagger that always made me uneasy, he boasted to everyone that he was betting on his son.

I threw the dice, rolled a four, and the men placed their bets.

My attention was focused on the dice lying in the ring when I heard Dad shout out, "You can't fade when my son throws the dice!" To fade was to bet that the shooter will lose.

I glanced up and saw him staring glassy-eyed and mean at the bootlegger. "You're a damn fool if you think I am going to let you fade," he said again.

The grizzled bootlegger stared straight back at Dad.

"You calling me a fool?" he said. "You may be Jim Wallace's boy, but you ain't no Jim Wallace." His voice was breaking with anger. I froze in place, hardly daring to breathe.

About the same size as my father, the bootlegger had blazing, bulging, dark brown eyes that showed no fear. He was wearing overalls without a shirt and the contracted musculature of his arms exposed the tension. Something bad was about to happen.

I watched helplessly as Dad's face faded from fury to fright. I had never seen that look on him before. The bootlegger bounded to his feet and so did Dad, their eyes locked. But I could tell that Dad had already lost this war of nerves. Suddenly, the bootlegger slapped my father on both sides of his face with a rapid back and forth motion using his right hand.

The bootlegger then turned in my direction. "I'm sorry that you have to watch this, son," he said to me. "But your father has been asking for this for a long time." My insides twisted.

Dad looked sick, as though he were ready to throw up. His head bent low and it seemed to me that he was pretending to be too drunk to respond. One step at a time, he backed up toward the car, the doors still wide open, the radio still blaring. With assured swagger, the bootlegger followed after him.

"You deserve this, Brady," he said. "I am going to teach you a lesson."

He began to slap Dad again—hard—first one cheek and then the other, pausing between slaps to allow Dad the chance to defend himself. But Dad submitted to the beating without resistance. His face turned increasingly red with each blow. For the first time, I saw my father as a fearful man. I felt sorry for him.

One of the other men finally persuaded the bootlegger to leave off.

Silently, Dad got into the front passenger seat of the car; I climbed behind the wheel, and the three others crammed into the back. As I drove, the bootlegger alternately lectured and challenged my father for the entire ride back to retrieve our car. Dad never once spoke.

Much later, when Dad and I were alone again on the road home, an awkward quiet filled the car. As I downshifted gears to make it up the final, steep hill, my father broke the silence.

"I could have beaten that man," he said. "You know that, don't you, son?"

By now, it was pitch black outside and a phalanx of night bugs was flying into the headlights of the car.

"I didn't want to get into a fight in front of my son," he continued.

I was glad for the jet-black night because it hid my tears. I wondered if I'd witnessed the reason why Dad so often came home an angry man.

CHAPTER ELEVEN

Burning Down the House

B y the time I started seventh grade, I was enrolled in yet another school, Center Point—an aged, wood-framed, two-room schoolhouse that my father had also attended when he was a boy. I continued to long for stability where there was none—not at school, not at home. Everything was chaotic and impermanent, except for the beauty of the landscape surrounding us. The wildness of the woods was, for me, more civilized than home, and it always welcomed me.

Dad had moved us into a house that he'd purchased for seven hundred and fifty dollars, owner financed with a small down payment. It was as neglected, primitive, and unwanted as all the others, but the family was excited because this was the first and only home our father ever bought. It stood solitary at the top of a very long, steep hill and looked like it had been vacant for years. The school bus driver was not too happy with our location and neither were my siblings and I. We were the first stop in the morning and the last drop-off in the afternoon, and we had to ride for an hour both ways. The old bus struggled mightily to climb our hill, inch by inch, its grinding transmission vibrating the floor beneath my seat. I winced at the straining gears and, each and every afternoon, felt guilty that the driver had to mount the hill just for us, especially on days when he betrayed his irritation. Going downhill in the morning, I knew, inflicted equal injury on the school bus brakes.

In the spring, our house burned down to the ground while I was at school.

When I stepped off the bus, I was shocked to see a heap of still-smoldering ashes and rubble where the house used to be. My first fear was for my family, but Mom was standing, unhurt, in the front yard holding in her arms my littlest brother, Brady. Her calm, capable face reassured me that everyone was okay. I could read Mom's face pretty well. I had learned my toughness from her.

By the end of the day, I heard the whole story from Bracy. Dad had planned the fire in order to collect on the insurance money. The dry wood and blistered paint of the old house had made the perfect tinder. That morning, Dad had ordered Bracy to stay home from school, wait until the bus had picked up the rest of us, and then build a fire in the hall closet. He directed Bracy to crumple up old newspaper and catalog pages, loosely stack the crumpled paper three feet deep in the closet, and then strike a match. The fire was ablaze in seconds and rapidly spread out of control.

Because Dad wanted the scene to appear authentic and accidental, he and Bracy didn't start throwing things out the windows and doors until after the fire was raging. They were able to rescue our few pieces of furniture and some clothes but couldn't save everything. None of my personal items—my fishing gear, work clothes, work shoes—survived the flames.

Dad never explained his actions, and burning down the house was no different. Bracy and I had several theories. The rent was past due, and when the rent was past due, Dad liked to cut and run. The insurance money this time would just sweeten the escape. We'd also overhead that Dad had a legal problem and needed to hire an attorney. A few months would go by before we found out the nature of this legal problem, but he did get the insurance money for the fire—we never knew how much—and he never got caught.

I figured that Bracy suffered the most from this episode. He didn't like setting fire to the house and felt guilty and ashamed about it, even though he was only following Dad's instructions. If it had been me rather than Bracy, I think helping to burn down our house would have ruined me for life. I couldn't have imagined living with that kind of fraud on my conscience. Surely, Mom knew the truth behind the fire. But she stayed silent about it. She was a survivor who picked her fights with my father very carefully. It would have been unwise for her to make an issue of it. Mom's priority had always been watching over her family, and, with Brady, there were seven of us now. She believed in prayer and prayed for her children. Mom prayed and Dad drank.

CHAPTER TWELVE

A Presence in the Woods

A few days after the fire, our family moved to an old house in Potneck, the area in Stewart County that my ancestors had settled and where a long line of Wallaces had grown up. The house stood on River Road, a narrow dirt and gravel road that ran parallel to the wide, winding Cumberland River, where we caught a lot of fish—perch, catfish, and crappie mostly. The front porch had sagged loose from the house, and when we sat there, I remember the occasional passing car whipping up dust clouds that settled on our clothes and faces. I could taste the dust. As with most of our places, there wasn't another house in sight.

After the move, Bracy attended a few church meetings, on weekends, in a large black-tarp tent that had been set up in an open field at the junction of Bumpus Mills Road and Highway 79. The church meetings, known as revivals, were common in Stewart County. Pastors traveled to remote, rural areas like Potneck from cities as far away as Nashville.

One Saturday, my brother asked me if I'd like to join him. I thought he was probably more interested in meeting girls than in anything else but wanted some company for the long three-mile walk to the meeting. Bracy was fifteen and in high school now and I welcomed the opportunity to spend time with him. I was honored that my older brother wanted me to come along. We walked two miles east on River Road and then another mile south on Bumpus Mills Road to where it joins Highway 79, the main route through Stewart County.

We arrived just as the sun was setting behind the trees and the sermon had begun. Bracy and I took a seat in the very back of the tent, which was lit with rows of hanging lightbulbs. Forty people or so were seated on folding chairs and listening to the pastor. A piano stood behind the pulpit and after the sermon a gray-haired woman led the congregation in the singing. Bracy made eye contact with a very cute girl across the aisle, while I watched and listened to what was going on under the tent. I had never been to a revival meeting before and didn't take it all that seriously, but I was impressed by the energy in the crowd. It was apparent that the pastor's wit was keen as a razor. His words seemed to tantalize the audience. He used the authority of the pulpit skillfully to pitch his practiced spiel.

By the time Bracy and I started home, it was quite dark and especially dark on the narrow road through the woods and marshes. We hadn't gone far when, walking next to Bracy, I felt the undeniable presence of something both inside and outside of me, permeating my being. I couldn't see anything but I felt as if my whole body was being touched with an infinite, almost unbearable tenderness. I had never felt this sensation, yet it felt completely familiar to me. It frightened me and soothed me at the same time. I hadn't been educated in any religion in my twelve years, nor had I ever read the Bible, but this invisible presence felt pure and holy—like love itself, like peace itself. I knew it loved. I knew it was love. I felt cradled in the arms of the universe. *This must be God*, I thought to myself. Painful waves of unworthiness welled up and I had the strong urge to cry. Silently, I began to pray, wondering if Bracy was experiencing the same thing.

"Do you feel something?" I asked him.

"No," he said. "Why?"

"Oh, nothing."

A few steps later, Bracy stopped and said, "I'll be back in a minute."

"Where are you going?"

"I'm just going to take a leak," he said and then disappeared beneath a small bridge off the road.

Grateful to be alone, I dropped to my knees, closed my eyes, and continued to pray, using the only words I knew from listening to my mother: "God forgive me, God help me, God forgive me, God help me," over and over again. The prayers calmed me some, but the anguish of guilt and unworthiness remained. I got up off my knees just as Bracy returned to the road and we walked on, me now lagging behind Bracy by five feet or so. I continued to pray in silence, feeling spellbound.

We had walked a mile and just turned left onto River Road when, looking toward a clearing in the woods on my right, I saw an enormous white light, otherworldly, and shining in the dark through the trees. About forty feet away and fifteen feet tall, it looked like a luminous oval moon, surrounded by an aura of gold. Incandescent, pulsating, this blaze of light was blinding, brighter than anything I had ever seen or imagined. Like an irresistible magnet, it drew me in. It was all consuming. I couldn't take my eyes away. I was anchored to the spot.

"Bracy, look," I called out. "What is that?"

Still walking five paces ahead, Bracy turned his head toward the left, away from the light to look at me, his eyes locked onto mine.

"Look over there!" I said, pointing. "Do you see that?"

But Bracy continued looking only at me. I turned to face the still-shimmering light that seemed alive somehow, a vortex of energy, radiating from its center the pure presence of unconditional love, the same presence that had come to me invisibly on the road a mile back. Soundlessly, with words beyond words, it communicated something directly to me—and only to me: *Everything will be all right.*

The unspoken essence of this message was as real to me as Bracy still standing there on River Road. I felt immediately and deeply calm and at peace. In my body, the heavy feelings of unworthiness dissolved. I felt light enough to fly, exhilarated, alive with hope. I felt immersed in the purity and love and vastness of a power greater than myself, a power I had no name for. I felt like the universe was my church.

All of a sudden, Bracy unaccountably took off running down the road. I ran after him. We ran all the way home. Even as I ran, I felt calm, gladdened, free from fear. I could feel my fists relax.

Before we fell asleep, Bracy and I discussed the incident very briefly. He told me that he was frightened when he turned around and saw my face.

"Your face . . . ," he said, his voice trailing off. We never spoke of it again.

The next morning, upon awakening, I still felt enveloped in the overwhelming love of the night before. To my surprise, it hadn't left me. I was overcome with joy and immediately began to cry. I then heard a knock at the front door. A minister from a church in Potneck was paying us a visit. I heard him tell Mom that he'd felt compelled to stop. Intuitively, I knew why he'd come, whether he knew it or not. I knew it had something to do with me. It wasn't a coincidence.

So I walked out of my bedroom and, kindly, the minister said to me, "You are the reason I am here." With his hands on my shoulder, he said, "Let us kneel and pray."

He told me that I had received the gift of knowledge and that I could never feign ignorance again. I needed to be baptized, he said. He promised to return to conduct the ceremony, which he did in early summer.

He baptized me in the Cumberland River at a place called Jackson's Landing. I remember the water being very cold. I remember it being a joyful experience. I knew very little about baptism and what it meant, but it felt like the right thing to do.

I wouldn't come to the realization until much later that my experience on that late-spring night in Potneck had changed me forever.

CHAPTER THIRTEEN

Father Goes to Jail

D ad's legal troubles eventually came to light. With a partner, he had committed a felony by stealing eleven rolls of
barbwire fencing from the stockyard of a local merchant.
The probability that he was facing jail time for the offense was strong
and of great concern. For days my mother and father discussed the
likelihood that she would have to support the family while he was
gone. As undependable as Dad was, as irregularly as he worked, he
did bring in some money from time to time. So Mom was troubled.
I heard her praying for help. As the trial date approached, the mood
in our household was gloomy, strained, and apprehensive.

On the day of the trial, we were all in the courtroom—Papa Jim
and Mamma Pearl, my aunts and uncles, and us. Mom, my brothers and sisters, and I sat in the front row and watched as Dad pled
guilty and stood before the judge to face sentencing. The judge took
his time reading aloud the details of Dad's crime. On June 25, 1962,
he was sentenced to six months of hard labor in the county jail in

Dover. The judge told Dad that he was giving him a break because of his family, who needed him at home. As the judge read the sentence, I could hear some of my aunts and uncles crying. I looked over at Mom and she was crying too. I watched as they led my father away in handcuffs. It was two days before Mom's thirty-sixth birthday.

With Dad in jail, the family had a half-year respite from the violence and abuse and chaos attending his drinking. As it turned out, because of Dad's incarceration, Mom was eligible for welfare assistance from the State of Tennessee. This was income we could count on, providing financial security, however slight, that we'd never known. For the first time in my young memory, we knew peace. Painful as it was to acknowledge, Dad's absence was giving us more than his presence.

As usual, Mom used the money wisely. As the weather turned colder, she even found enough to purchase firewood sometimes, which freed Bracy and me up to study or just spend time with the family. One activity we filled some of our free time with was the game I Spy, which Mom had taught us. In the game, a player is designated as *It* and hides an object in a room—we used the front room—leaving the tiniest portion exposed so the object can be found. The other players filter into the room and begin to hunt, asking "Am I hot or cold?" as they search. Once a player spots the object, the player calls out "I spy" and whispers the location in Its ear. All players must find the object before the game is over.

Dad was released from jail around Christmastime. He moved us back to Big Rock, in a house we'd once rented, and our interlude of financial security and domestic peace was at an end. Life resumed as it had ever been.

CHAPTER FOURTEEN

Turning the Other Cheek

After I was baptized, I began attending the minister's church, a clapboard building painted milk-white and dating back to the late 1800s. On Sundays, the minister would pick me up and drop me off. Going to church, however, I soon discovered that there's a price to be paid for trying to follow in the footsteps of Christ. You have to give up the sins of the world—and they are everywhere.

Many days I prayed for the strength to live up to Christ's example. But I soon became confused. In a few short months, I had formed the belief that in order to lead a Christian life and to hold on to the gift of the night in Potneck, I had to live a perfect life—a life free of sin, free of a single bad thought. But, once school resumed in the fall—my final year in middle school—I had a serious problem adjusting to the philosophy of "turning the other cheek." At six years old, I'd had my first lesson in fighting, in standing up to bullies. I had learned that it was the wise course of action. But now, I was being encouraged to choose a purer, more pacifist course. The only problem was that my eighth-grade peers showed no respect toward my new behavior and seemed to take particular pleasure in tormenting me daily. They were heartless. Picking on someone like me who was a known fighter was the kind of ego boost these guys could only dream about. I was a sitting duck. I was pushed, punched, and bullied until I dropped swiftly to the bottom of the pecking order. If you were a boy, you fought while attending school in Stewart County. If you didn't fight, you got beaten up, not badly, but beaten up nonetheless.

Week after week, I refused to fight no matter the provocation. For the first time in my life, I knew what it felt like to be a continuing victim of bullies. Each encounter wound me a notch tighter until, one day, I snapped and surrendered to the desire to defend myself.

A boy at school, a perpetually surly, mocking bully, had been jabbing at my arm during breaks—a typical, thickheaded test of my courage. It was incomprehensible to me. Jab after jab, he was hitting a person who clearly only wanted peace. My anger built as, over and over, my desire for peace was mistaken as a sign of fear and weakness. One day I reacted. This hefty boy had chosen the wrong fight on the wrong day. I exploded and fought back. I beat up the classmate in front of everyone.

When it was over, I felt relief and horror in equal measure. Home from school, I crawled behind the couch and prayed earnestly for forgiveness for what I had done. On the dark road that night in Potneck, I felt like I had stepped into a whole new possibility for my life. Now, I feared that, by fighting, I'd lost that promise, perhaps forever. Despondent and conflicted, I suffered terribly.

The following morning, the guilt of the fight persisted. My body felt like a stone. But as the day wore on, as the intensity eased, I could feel my connection to a power greater than myself still intact and strong. I was flooded with gratitude at this realization. The Potneck experience could not be taken away from me. It hadn't abandoned me. The gift was still mine. I wanted desperately to hold on to the purity of that experience. I felt, somehow even then, that my life depended on it. The phrase "Everything will be all right" became like a prayer that was praying me. It soothed and stilled my insides.

For the rest of the school year, I continued to fight when necessary. I was beginning to believe that a flawless life was not possible but, rather, something to aspire to. At thirteen, I fought more often than any member of my family. Even Bracy was no match for me. But from that time on, I never fought without a heavy heart.

CHAPTER FIFTEEN

The Secret Room

I n June of 1963, I graduated from eighth grade. Early that summer, the summer before high school, I badly wanted some privacy—to be left alone, to pray, to savor the silence.

Behind our house was a wide field of very tall grass, probably five feet high. I built a secluded, well-hidden shelter in the center of that field, about a quarter-mile from home. For the walls, I used plastic milk-crates, for a thatched roof, twigs and hay, and for the floor, I cut a swath of long grass to serve as straw, making the room soft and comfortable. At six by eight feet, the room was spacious and big enough to lie down in. Finally, I had a room of my own, and I loved it. It was my refuge and my favorite hangout for the entire summer. I could leave the world behind. And it was a secret. No one in the family knew about it until the day that my sister Faye, fourteen, confided in me that she was thinking of running away from home. She didn't say why and I didn't ask. I told her about my secret hiding place. I suggested it to her as an alternative to running away. She agreed and we spent the day making improvements. As safety was her major concern, we stacked heavy rocks around the perimeter, hung a tin plate at the entrance, and strewed dry leaves all around the outside so she would hear anyone's approach.

Faye was so pleased she decided that she would run away from home that very night. As the sun went down, I left my shelter for supper and told Faye that I'd come back later on with a plate of food. I had been home for only a few minutes when Faye casually and innocently entered the house and sat down on our ratty couch.

"What are you doing here?" I whispered. She told me that after I left it grew dark, she got scared, and decided not to run away after all. When I expressed my surprise that she hadn't tried it even for a night, she said that if I liked my secret room so much, why didn't I just stay overnight there myself.

After having made it nice for her, I was disappointed, but she never betrayed the existence of my hiding place. As far as anyone knew, I was in the woods somewhere, rather than sitting in my secret refuge in the field for hours praying, meditating, and enjoying the solitude. My prayers were very simple. I prayed for mercy. For all my flaws, I was seeking pardon. Meditation came naturally to me but not as easily. From as far back as Granite City, when I was six, I'd been practicing a form of meditation without knowing it. To withstand my father's rages, I would close my eyes, relax my body, and focus on the words "it never happened," which brought me peace and enabled me to keep my sanity. Now, in the privacy of my room in the grass, my meditation consisted of those same things and also a mantra that I created for myself and repeated over and over to myself silently. This would take me to a place of rest where the only thing I could feel was my breathing, which was my anchor. If I could control my breathing, I could control my mind. But I had to practice, I had to be alone and, initially, I needed darkness. The thatched roof darkened my space considerably, and provided protection from the sun.

Frequently, my meditation had to do with envisioning a future without poverty and violence. If it hadn't been for Mom, we would probably all have run away at one time or another.

For me that summer, escaping poverty became not a dream but a quest. The seed of pure possibility had been planted in Potneck.

PART TWO

Nashville

CHAPTER SIXTEEN

Nashville with an Edge

I n early 1964, right after New Year's, Dad moved us to Nashville, eighty-five miles southeast of Stewart County. The year before, Mom had had another baby, Timmy, the first of us not to be born at home, who expanded our family to eight—six boys and two girls. Eight children meant more pressure on Dad to work. The best job opportunities were to be found in Nashville, he said. I harbored serious doubts about a new location making any difference to his ways, but we dared not question the move, for which we were utterly unprepared.

We settled into a small, low-rent apartment on a street called Trinity Lane in East Nashville, which lay on the other side of the Cumberland River from downtown Nashville. Everything about Nashville except for living by the Cumberland again was a radical change for us, especially its size. All of Stewart County could have fit neatly within Nashville's borders. And while all of Stewart County had fewer than eight thousand people, the single city of Nashville had more than a hundred and seventy thousand. For us, this was a big city. We were used to living off the land. Here, there wasn't any land to live off of. There were no plots for a vegetable garden. Nor could Mom gather us together to seek protection in the woods if things got too violent at home.

How we were going to survive concerned me, but I wasn't completely resistant to the move. By this time I had become interested in job opportunities for myself and was optimistic that I'd find something in the city. Back in Stewart County, I'd helped Dad on a job digging a plumbing trench a hundred feet long and three feet deep. We worked two twelve-hour days one weekend and on Sunday night Dad had given me five dollars as my share of the earnings, a small fortune to me. I liked the feeling. It whetted my appetite for earning money.

In Nashville, our new place offered the luxuries of indoor plumbing and heating. Not only did this mean we didn't have to use an outhouse or the out-of-doors for a toilet, but more importantly, Bracy and I were relieved of the obligation of hauling water and supplying firewood for the family. That meant more time for other things.

We hadn't been long on Trinity Lane before I realized we were living in a rough neighborhood with a criminal attitude. The street bore all the signs—trashy yards and junk cars parked on the street; men and teenagers hanging out, shirts off, beers in hand, and staring down passing cars; foul language coming from open windows; battered faces on women. Local hoodlums were involved in stealing cars, breaking and entering, and other crimes of opportunity. Booze, sniffing glue, and teenage sex were common and, at night and on weekends, tough street kids hung out on corners looking for a fight. Trinity Lane boys liked to brag about their successes, so whenever I ran into them, I'd hear all the details. They were felons in the making. Over time, I watched each one of them get busted by the police.

It took me a while to adjust, and I knew I had choices to make. To help me with this, I tapped into the message from Potneck: Everything will be all right. Expecting that all would be well seemed, naturally, to turn me toward good choices rather than bad. Sometimes the message dropped into my consciousness by itself when needed. Other times I had to choose to remember it. Either way, it was the star I was trying to steer by. It helped me to anticipate consequences, and I knew that whenever I made a wrong choice, I paid the too-heavy price of guilt.

CHAPTER SEVENTEEN

Putting the Issue of Poverty in Perspective

F ocusing on finding a job greatly helped me to escape the temptations, pressures, and violence of the street corner. Very soon after arriving in Nashville, I started looking after school and on weekends for part-time work. I completed job applications at every business establishment within a two-mile radius of our home. I was stunned to find so many businesses so close by and so close together. I applied at restaurants, garages, grocery stores, retail shops, and other vendors in the neighborhood.

Unfortunately, I naively told them my real age not realizing there were laws restricting the hiring of kids under sixteen. No doubt, the majority of small business owners wouldn't have cared that I was underage as long as I could do the work, but they couldn't knowingly put me on the payroll. Had I simply stated at the outset that I was sixteen, my applications, most likely, would have been considered. So I had to get creative.

One Saturday in February, I noticed a pickup truck loaded with firewood traveling slowly down the street in front of our apartment. The next weekend the same pickup came by again, this time making a stop at the end of the block. I watched as an old man got out of the truck and sold a basketful of firewood to a woman at the door. He walked sluggishly and seemed like he was struggling to carry the load. The following weekend I waited again for the old man and his truck. Instinct told me that if this man were interested in hiring someone, he wouldn't be worrying about the fact that I was underage. If he needed help hefting his firewood, I thought, I was the expert he could count on. I knew everything there was to know about firewood and I'd carried heavy loads of it all kinds of distances. When he reappeared this time, I ran after the truck for two blocks until its next stop. As the old man lumbered out of his pickup, I said to him, "Mister, could you give me a job?"

"You willing to work for five bucks a day, son?" he asked, after a moment.

My response was immediate. "Yes, sir!"

I started work right then, immensely pleased with earning a salary for work I had already been doing most of my life. Plus, the work was only on weekends so it wouldn't interfere with school.

My new employer was overweight and looked unhealthy. He wore dirty, shoulder-length hair that was never combed. He sweated constantly, even though it was winter, and he quickly lost his breath when lifting a basketful of wood. He looked over seventy, but I wondered if he wasn't younger. His dry, ruddy face and poor health suggested he had lived a hard life.

The old man's business strategy was simple. On weekends he purchased a truckload of discounted firewood at a lumberyard on the outskirts of Nashville, and then sold it in the city for three dollars a basket. His aging, black Ford pickup had a modified truck bed that enabled it to haul more than double the amount of wood the truck was designed to carry. The old man had nailed planks and boards together to create a truck bed over seven feet high with a platform that extended over the top of the cab. He sold his wood in the poorest neighborhoods of East Nashville, where many of the residents used pot-bellied stoves to heat their homes. Each wicker basket of wood held about six split logs, which provided sufficient fuel to keep a woodstove burning for four hours.

As he drove slowly up and down each street, the old man called out, "Wood man! Wood man!" He'd pause between announcements to listen attentively for an interested customer. Inside the truck, the heater blasted hot air on my legs and feet, but my arms were freezing because the old man kept the windows rolled down. He had a habit of constantly rubbing his left arm with his right hand as he steered. We rarely conversed during our workday. All day long we drove the streets, until the truck was empty, no matter how many hours it took.

When a voice shouted back, "Here, wood man!" the old man braked. My job was to jump out of the passenger seat, run up to the customer, and find out how much wood was needed. Often, customers would simply hold up their fingers to indicate the number of baskets they wanted, which saved me a trip to the door. Quickly, I then loaded a basket with wood, carried it into the home, and stacked the wood as directed.

After I started working for him, the old man rarely bothered to get out of the truck, except to make repairs when it broke down, which it often did. The shock absorbers had long since worn out. And the engine made a chronic knocking sound that the old man attributed to poor oil gaskets, so he frequently stopped to add oil. The truck itself, with all its cranky noises and the black smoke from its exhaust, was enough to announce our presence on a street, but the old man continued to call out "Wood man!" as he'd done every weekend for ten years.

Working at this job shocked me in many ways. I saw families whose financial situation was as bad as ours had been in Stewart County, and some worse. Poverty in the city doesn't have the solace of the countryside or fresh air like we'd had. In the cramped apartments I saw in East Nashville, mothers hung bedsheets from the windows and doors to keep their living rooms warm, like Mom had done in winter back home. The difference was that our houses, though dilapidated, were never sealed tight; cracks in the wood-planked floors and walls let in the cold, but also let in fresh air and light. In the rundown city apartments I entered, the hanging sheets darkened the room and were themselves stained charcoal-gray from the wood smoke of the fire in the stove. Inside the gloomy, closed rooms, the air was uncomfortably smoky and unhealthy. Some of the places seemed unfit for occupancy; the living conditions were deplorable. I felt most sorry for the children. I knew what they were going through and it made me sad to witness it. The majority of the customers were black, mostly women alone at home with children.

On one particularly cold day, midway through our route, I heard the voice of a woman cry out, "Here, wood man! Here!" She pointed at the truck bed and said, "We need all the wood you've got." I filled a basket and followed her into her apartment, where I noticed a girl about my own age sitting on the floor by a sheet-covered window in dingy gray light. The girl had on a white nightgown, which contrasted nicely against her dark black skin. I remember thinking how pretty she looked. Our eyes met briefly and she turned away. I looked around the room and saw that there were other children sitting on mattresses spread out across the floor. There was no other furniture in the room. The woman directed me to pile the wood next to a small pot-bellied stove in the corner. The room was very cold and I asked permission to start the fire. I made a dozen trips in order to completely unload the truck. When I had finished, the woman told me she only had twelve dollars. That was twenty-four dollars less than was owed for the twelve baskets of wood. "Don't worry about it," I said.

I returned to the truck and handed the twelve dollars to the old man. I told him that I hadn't charged her for all the baskets. "There are small children freezing to death in there," I said.

Angry, the old man refused to pay me for the whole weekend of work. I thought he was going to fire me, and I didn't care if he did.

Instead, he changed the rules. Thereafter, customers had to pay the old man in advance before I was allowed to unload the wood.

A couple of weeks later, just before spring, the old man discontinued his wood business due to his failing health. He didn't bother to tell his customers that the service would be stopped. He had made the decision to quit the business and that was the end of it.

In addition to the ten dollars a weekend I earned from the job, my perspective on poverty had been changed. We were poor, but it was clear to me now that we were not alone, and there were people in East Nashville worse off than we were.

CHAPTER EIGHTEEN

A Family in Crisis

During the eight weeks I worked with the old wood man, Dad changed jobs twice. For the first few years in Nashville, he mainly drove a cab for minimum wage and tips. This was a time before computers, so his past hadn't followed him and he managed to get a taxi license. I think he worked for every cab company in Nashville at one time or another and was fired by all of them. He was an alcoholic cab driver in a city loaded with beer joints and whiskey bars. That particular job gave him the transportation and freedom to do whatever he wanted to do, whenever he wanted to do it. He continued to drink and rage and abuse Mom.

Bracy, Faye, and I were enrolled in Cohn High School, which was a quantum leap in size from the one- and two-room schoolhouses in Stewart County, but I was older now and not so intimidated. The high school was only a fifteen-minute walk from the apartment, unlike the sometimes hour-long school bus rides back in Stewart County. I liked the fact that I could walk to school and also that no one singled me out there for being poor. Cohn had its share of fights, but I wasn't part of that culture. Even though I was an experienced fighter by that time, even though I had racked up more fistfights than most men accumulate in a lifetime, guys at school left me alone after the first week because they knew I would fight back. All it took was one fight to gain a high rank in the pecking order. If someone threw the first punch, they were in for a serious fight because I would fight to win. During my teenage years, I rarely lost a fistfight.

The streets were another matter. Walking home from school or work I might have to fight a drunk, adult or teenage, who wouldn't leave me alone. The behavior of kids high on glue was unpredictable. I saw kids sucker-punch their best friends, without provocation, in intoxicated rages. To protect myself, I had to learn to read the people on the street and decide my route accordingly. If I found myself in an unavoidable fight, I'd take on the toughest kid in a group. If you take on the weakest member, then he becomes the underdog and you risk having all of them jump on you at once. Whether you win or lose, fighting the big guy earns you respect in the neighborhood.

I missed the woods and hills and creeks of Stewart County, but Nashville offered a different and better kind of freedom. I went from living in an isolated, rural area where my father was able to hold us captive in house after house—with no access to public transportation whatsoever—to a wide open city with a big bus system and plenty of jobs. Two bus stops stood just around the corner from the apartment, one on Gallatin Road, the other on Dickerson. That I could hop on a bus to take me wherever I needed to go was a revelation—and also necessary for finding and keeping a job. I liked school and did my schoolwork, but my primary focus was on paid work—not on school sports, not on making friends at school or on the streets, not on dating, not even on home life or its inconveniences, like the fact that I was still sharing a bed with Bracy, Steve, and Rick. My first year in Nashville was all about mastering my new surroundings and earning money after school and on weekends to help the family and support myself. I got mobile fast and liked being out from under my father's gaze and alcoholism.

After the wood man, I found work as a short-order cook at Shoney's Big Boy Restaurant and sacked groceries at H. G. Hill. On weekends, I also had a job doing yard maintenance for an apartment building near Vanderbilt University on the other side of the river. I had to transfer buses, but fifty cents got me to work and back. The landscaping aspects of that job appealed to me, trimming hedges and planting flowers. I cleaned the apartment grounds during the day and worked as a factory janitor at night. The buses stopped rolling after eleven, so when I finished work at midnight, I'd have a few miles to walk home.

By that point I had learned to tell all prospective employers, when asked, that I was sixteen.

At home, it wasn't long before we found ourselves with little or no food again and the gas and electric being turned off for nonpayment. For the first time, Mom appealed to the local welfare agency, which provided some temporary relief in those areas. Mom worried about the fact that her fifty-five-dollar monthly federal government check would be ending as soon as her eldest child, Bracy, turned eighteen, which was less than a year away. It was a pittance, but it was a pittance we could count on.

Bracy and I both contributed money toward the support of the family, but our part-time earnings weren't enough to solve the myriad problems. Bracy was a gifted auto mechanic and did that for a while. We lived in a low-rent neighborhood, but even so, our living expenses were higher than they'd been in Stewart County, and we had no immediate family nearby as a safety net.

In late spring, before the end of his junior year, Bracy decided to quit high school and take a full-time job parking cars in downtown Nashville. The money would provide a financial boost, but I found it painful to see him stop short of graduating. I feared the negative consequences of being a high school dropout for him down the road.

The family survived on a day-to-day basis, never knowing what would happen next. Without reliable income, there was the real threat of Child Social Services taking custody of us. Someone had to take the main responsibility for supporting the family, and it wasn't going to be Dad. So, toward summer, Mom decided to go to work. She discussed the problem with Faye and asked her to drop out of school, too, in order to take care of one-year-old Timmy and three-year-old Brady. Rick was in elementary school, Donna and Steve in middle school. Faye agreed and quit high school after finishing her sophomore year. I felt like my family was collapsing under the weight of poverty and there was nothing that I could do about it.

Shortly afterward, Mom found a full-time job as a welder at Field Crutcher Wire Company on Dickerson Road in East Nashville near the Cumberland Bridge earning the minimum wage of $1.25 an hour. Her presence at home during the day was sorely missed. She was our anchor and pillar of stability and held us together as a family unit. She managed the crises, financial and otherwise. Whenever one of us had a problem or needed to express an emotion, we always knew that Mom would be there to listen and to respond wisely and with love. She provided the energy that made the family cohesive and strong. And thanks to her unbiased mothering—no favorites—there was trust and cooperation among the children. When conflicts arose, she was the one who offered solutions.

For the first time in our lives, the eight of us were home alone, and there was no one to manage differences or help us deal with our individual day-to-day problems, although Faye did her best.

Dad was rarely around and when he did show up, he was usually drunk, drifting in and out of alcoholic binges from week to week. During brief periods of sobriety, he'd drive a cab or pick up odd jobs painting or carpentering or doing manual labor. For the first time,

Mom swore out warrants against him for his physical abuse. I think she finally came to believe that he might go further. Also, I think she was letting Bracy and me know that the situation was in the hands of the law now and that we should stay out of it. More than once, my brother and I had talked about beating up Dad and running him off. But we needed Mom's permission to do that, which, too fearful of the consequences, she would never have given.

After that, the police came to our house regularly. My father would plead for mercy and they would let him off the hook almost every time. I'd be a long block away, see police cars heading toward our building, and run home knowing it was my father beating up on Mom. By the time I arrived, he would be in handcuffs in the front yard, the police admonishing him, my father offering pathetic excuses, which made me cringe. The coda to the nightmare was watching the police drive off and then having to hear my father gloating to Mom. Many times, it was more than I could stand. Sometimes I'd even get mad at my mother. *Let your boys kick his butt or divorce him*, I thought.

My father had stopped laying a hand on Mom whenever Bracy and I were around. My brother was more apprehensive about taking him on because he thought a fight between them would ruin his relationship permanently with Dad. But I had stopped caring about what my father thought of me long before. I wanted him gone. I was a ticking time bomb, and it was best for me to avoid him as much as possible.

Our first summer in Nashville, I turned fifteen. I'd come to know many guys in the neighborhood who had criminal records, many who had appeared more than once before a juvenile court judge. They talked about warnings from the judge and the probability that they would be seeing him again. Indeed, they predicted their own fate as repeat criminals, and laughed about a life destined to be spent behind bars. That kind of talk confused me. I couldn't understand how someone could simply give up on his future.

I learned things from the streets. I learned that the social dynamics in a poor neighborhood were likely to descend to the lowest common denominator. People can rise to expectations, but they can also sink to them. Kids old enough to think about it seemed to have little regard for higher education. Almost nobody planned for college. In fact, most kids—girls and boys—anticipated dropping out of high school in their junior year. Crime, violence, addiction, and no hope were accepted as a way of life. I came to know many of the victims and most of the perpetrators.

When your peers are downgrading the importance of achievement, it can be difficult to maintain a positive attitude about your future. Many times in East Nashville I isolated myself and prayed for the strength to persevere. When I felt myself slipping into despair, I reached for my strength: Everything will be all right. Those five simple words, when called upon, never ceased to show me the way forward and the way out, to put solid ground under me when it felt like quicksand.

CHAPTER NINETEEN

Lessons on Value and Social Class

I survived both my father and my neighborhood by keeping busy. At the beginning of my sophomore year, in the fall, I accepted a weekend job as a door-to-door salesman for a magazine distributor. I was grouped with ten other teenage boys. Each of us was dropped off on a different residential block in East Nashville and instructed to go to each door and attempt to sell a magazine subscription. Although I now had eight months of job experience behind me, none of it was in sales. I had no idea how to sell. So, without any training, I was rejected at each sales call.

At the end of the day the manager fired everyone who didn't sell at least one subscription. Those of us who were terminated received no money for our efforts. The ad in the newspaper had promised minimum wage for a day's work, but the manager informed us we didn't deserve to be paid.

This served as a lesson about value. The company was dishonest about the compensation. However, the reason I hadn't been paid was that my efforts were of no value to the company. After that experience, I made certain that I could provide value before I agreed to take on a job.

Setting a record low for our family, we moved only four times during my freshman and sophomore years. We mostly stayed in the Trinity Lane neighborhood, so I was able to continue at the same high school. My mother continued to work as a welder at the wire company on Gallatin Road.

And so it went during my freshman and sophomore years: time swept by, uncaring and cold, not sparing a single appraising glance at the chaos in my life. To get through my days, I stayed focused on hard work, week after week, job after job. My body went through the motions of going to school but I have very few memories of actually being there; not an image of the school building, or the name of a single teacher or even one friend. I didn't fit in with the middle-class students at school and I didn't want to be friends with the troublemakers on Trinity Lane. I lacked knowledge of the rules that govern the daily vernacular and behavior of middle-class students. For example, my language was casual, often laced with grammatical errors and slang, and I was more aggressive in my personality, which was the way we communicated in my neighborhood.

The middle-class students at school seemed uncomfortable with my behavior and I could tell they were deliberately avoiding me. To me, they seemed to be putting on airs, and though I tried very hard to mingle with this group, I was never successful at it during my high school years. Not knowing the rules isolated me from the mainstream society that I desperately wanted to join. Were it not for the shining light, that beacon that guides wayward souls, I would have surely given up. Like a star in the night, my light shined brightest when hope faltered in the darkest of moments. The message that everything will be all right would force me to stop the self-pity, to pick myself up from the bottom, and get up to face the day and try it all over again.

CHAPTER TWENTY

A Means to Escape

I n the summer after my sophomore year, I got my first full-time job as a uniformed parking lot attendant for a lot on Fourth Avenue in Nashville's downtown business district. I didn't have a driver's license, but the manager knew Bracy and offered me a job anyway. Bracy was working at a parking lot a few blocks away.

My starting pay was $1.65 an hour. The cost of my dark blue logo-jacket was taken out of my first paycheck.

From day one, the manager trained me in the art and science and secrets of parking cars, which would stand me in good stead.

After several days of training, I could back a car into a tight parking space with finesse. I became an expert at handling cash and ensuring the security of the automobiles, and I seemed to have a knack for pleasing the customers, which not only enhanced my standing with the management but also increased the frequency and amount of my tips. I wasn't reticent about engaging anyone in easy conversation. My success got me to thinking that there is no such thing as a bad job—it's what you put into the job that makes it rewarding.

Partway through the summer, I took on extra work on Friday and Saturday nights as a parking valet for the Grand Ole Opry. Most of our customers were Opry ticket holders, but some were the night's performers. One country music star drove a new Cadillac covered from bumper to bumper with gleaming silver dollars. The interior was sheepskin, and the dashboard was covered in more silver dollars. I loved sitting inside and driving that car and imagining myself having the kind of money that could afford such a vehicle.

At that time, the Grand Ole Opry was located at 115 Fifth Avenue North in the Ryman Auditorium. Directly across the street from the front entrance was the parking garage, which could hold no more than twenty cars at a time. The automobiles of the performing artists and other celebrities took priority and got parked inside the private garage. All other cars, unbeknownst to their owners, were driven right out the back exits of the garage to various other parking lots, some several blocks away.

I parked the cars of stars like Minnie Pearl, June Carter, and Buck Owens, but I possessed little to no interest in celebrity at the time. I was absorbed in my sole purpose for being there—retrieving their vehicles at full sprint and earning tips. The Grand Ole Opry was just another building to me, a means to an end, an opportunity to make money for the family.

After one night's performance, a customer handed me his claim ticket. Both he and his female companion were pretty drunk. In his mid-forties, the man was dressed in typical country music–star fashion—flashy bolo tie, bright-colored shirt with a big collar, and a fancy short-waisted leather jacket that matched perfectly with his expensive and tight-fitting tan slacks. His cowboy hat was custom-made, the brim laced with embroidery. I assumed he must have performed at the Opry that night, though I didn't recognize him.

The garage was crowded with two hundred Opry fans anxious to leave the premises. Fortunately, the color of this man's claim ticket told me his car was parked close at hand in the garage. He owned a new, flashy pink Cadillac, which I promptly retrieved and delivered to the gentleman and his lady, a gorgeous brunette wearing a low-cut western blouse and a short leather skirt, exposing tall, tanned legs in high, western-style leather boots.

"Son, do you think she's pretty?" the man said to me. He must have noticed I was staring at her.

I didn't know how to respond, so I said nothing. I was embarrassed that he'd noticed I was looking at her cleavage.

"Go ahead, son, you can touch them if you want," he said. The expression on his face suggested he was serious. I turned and began to walk away. He called out to me, "Wait, you forgot your tip!" When I turned back, he handed me a ten-dollar bill.

I opened the door for the woman and she smiled. She seemed to be enjoying my embarrassment. I heard them laughing as their car pulled away, both enjoying a big laugh at my expense. But I didn't mind. I was enjoying the ten-dollar tip.

In August, I moved to another full-time valet parking position at the Cain Sloan Department Store, the premier department store in Nashville. It was a step up in pay for me. Bracy was already working there and the manager had asked him to recruit me to work for them.

The pay was $1.95 an hour, plus an incentive bonus of ten cents for every parked car over seventy-two vehicles. My immediate objective was to take advantage of the incentive bonus and to get to the seventy-two-parked-car mark as quickly as possible each day, even if it meant running from car to car for eight hours, giving up my breaks and most of my lunch hour. This was a five-story garage that required us to ride a continuous pulley-driven lift, big enough for one person only, to travel up and down between floors efficiently. It was the responsibility of the rider to determine the safest jumping-on and jumping-off point. Skill on riding the descending lift was key to speeding up your rate of parking cars—as was running from a just-parked car to the lift and then from the lift to a car waiting to be parked. Careful, swift driving up the ramp didn't hurt either.

For the first two weeks, I followed this accelerated course of action and, on payday, my check reflected a bonus. I was rather proud of my accomplishment and made the mistake of telling my coworkers the exact amount of my paycheck. To my naive surprise, they didn't quite share in the joy. On the contrary, they were upset with me. My extra income had been earned at their expense, they believed. Only so many cars came into the garage on a given day; therefore, each attendant should be entitled to an equal percentage. The incident caused such a disturbance that the manager was compelled to arrange a meeting. As a result, he created a new rule that essentially did away with the incentive pay, so in the end, all that hustle and extra effort backfired on me.

Lesson learned: One person's success can be perceived as another's loss. Productivity is more important to some people than others. Those same people for whom productivity is not so important are often green-eyed with envy when someone else makes money.

The experience soured my experience at Cain Sloan's parking concession. I gave two weeks' notice, planning to find another parking job in the evenings and on weekends once school resumed. But two days after giving notice I was involved in an accident.

Retrieving a parked car, as I started down the narrow, winding ramp that led from the roof to the first floor of the garage, I discovered the brakes didn't work. The car started to pick up speed and I tried pulling on the emergency brake. No go. I gripped the steering wheel as the car, unbridled, screeched down the concrete ramp. In seconds, I was on the second floor and zooming toward the first, where customers were waiting in line, unaware of the runaway vehicle headed in their direction. I had to make a quick decision: the customers or the concrete wall that lay straight ahead. I chose the wall.

I was told later that the noise could be heard blocks away as I smashed head-on into the concrete wall. The hood crumpled up like tin. The engine landed in the passenger seat. A cloud of dust and smoke filled the inside of the car. I was dazed. I felt someone grab my right arm and begin to pull me from the car.

"Doug, are you okay?" I recognized my brother's voice.

"Yeah, I think so."

He helped me to lie down right there on the garage floor.

"Just stay down, don't move," he said.

It took me a while to realize that I had been in an accident. Everything in my body had been jolted and I felt confused. I had been shaken up pretty badly and had bruises, but otherwise, as it turned out, I was basically unharmed.

The big boss from Cain Sloan got involved right away. He didn't know I was only sixteen and didn't have a driver's license. He showed genuine concern for me and assured me that I would be given medical care. He demanded an immediate meeting with the manager before storming back to his office.

The manager came back an hour later and gave me two weeks' pay. He told me to take off for the rest of my time with the company. I think they would have given me anything I asked for at that point, just to get me to go away.

CHAPTER TWENTY-ONE

Back to Stewart County

Papa Jim died of a massive heart attack that summer. We all went to Big Rock for the funeral, all ten of us packed into one of Dad's old cars for the hour-and-a-half ride up to Stewart County. Papa Jim had been the patriarch of the Wallace clan and his going was, for us, like the grandest tree in the forest being felled. He liked his moonshine, but it was never at a cost to his family. He had been a keen fighter, but had nothing left to prove. I never saw him lose his temper. He had the patience and calloused hands of a farmer and the long gaze of someone who's seen far. People listened to him. He loved his family, especially his sons, and he treated me like a son. I was going to miss him. He left a big footprint.

As the apple from the tree, my father couldn't have fallen farther, but I could tell the loss of Papa Jim affected him deeply. He'd loved his father, of that I had no doubt, and he grieved with the bottle.

In the fall, I returned to Cohn High School as a junior. I started the year with new clothes purchased from my summer earnings, so I was feeling good about that.

I also bought clothes and school supplies for Steve and Rick, who were still in middle school. And I lined up an after-school job at a placed called Maxine's Diner. I was feeling hopeful and confident that I'd be able to finish high school and apply to college.

It was an auspicious beginning for me, personally, but tensions at the high school were running high. A few weeks before, in early August, the Watts riots had exploded in Los Angeles. At school, all the kids were talking about it. For those of us living in Nashville's poorest neighborhoods, it had been obvious all summer that racial tension was reaching a boiling point. Six months earlier, Martin Luther King had organized the historic march from Selma to Mont-gomery, Alabama. Two weeks prior, another civil rights march to Montgomery was met with state troopers, tear gas, and billy clubs. Montgomery is fewer than three hundred miles from Nashville. Emo-tions were high. In East Nashville, word got out that white kids were being attacked and beaten up by black kids. I was aware of my own vulnerability and did my best to stay out of harm's way. I supported the struggle for civil rights, for which I caught some measure of grief from a minority of my white classmates in the form of ugly name-calling. For the most part, though, poor whites were in sympathy with the black cause. I thought the changes were necessary. I just had to take care not to be in the wrong place at the wrong time.

It was 1965, the same year that President Lyndon Baines John-son sent American combat troops and bombs into Vietnam for the first time. Young men turning eighteen were resentful of the military service being forced upon them by the draft. This was a big topic of conversation at school, too, and college students were publicly burn-ing their draft cards in protest of both compulsory service and the war. Congress responded swiftly by passing a law making it illegal to burn draft cards. Bracy had just turned eighteen in January and I was worried about him. For myself, draft age was two years away.

I remember a lot of powerful music was being written around this time. My favorite that fall was the Rolling Stones's "I Can't Get No Satisfaction," which captured the highly dissatisfied and disaffected mood of my generation. The song soared to the top of the charts. I'd always been drawn to music, and never more so than then.

Shortly after school began, I had an exchange of words, more heated than usual, with my father. He and Mom were in the kitchen, where he was harassing her for the way she was preparing his sandwich. I was standing at the hall doorway.

"I don't like the way you're treating Mom," I said.

His face turned blood red. I faced him squarely, looking unblinkingly into his eyes.

"Who do you think you are? Don't you talk to me like that," he said. He took a few steps in my direction.

"I'll whip your ass," he said.

"I'll take my chances if you want to try that," I said calmly.

He eased off, but I could tell he was upset, and not out of sadness at the thought of fighting a son. At times I thought he would have been more comfortable killing me than losing a fight to me.

We never mentioned it again.

Then, in October, my father informed me that I would be moving back to Stewart County to live with Mamma Pearl. He said that my Grandmother Wallace had been devastated by the death of Papa Jim and was afraid of being alone. My aunts and uncles were concerned for her safety, so they suggested to their brother, Brady, that he send one of his sons to stay with her. Dad chose me for the assignment.

Initially, I refused to go. I loved Mamma Pearl, but I loved my immediate family more. I didn't want to leave Nashville—not my family, not the opportunities, not my newfound mobility. I said no and tried to stand my ground against my father. He stormed out of the apartment warning me to have my bags packed by the time he returned, which I did.

While I packed, I thought of Mamma Pearl and how she needed someone to be with her. Though I wanted to stay in Nashville, in the end, it came down to my inner voice telling me to go and surrendering, once more, to the belief that everything would be all right.

I left almost immediately, but before going, I used my savings to buy more clothes for Stewart County—there wouldn't be any stores for a while—and I treated the family to a home-cooked, farewell steak dinner. Only none of us knew how to cook a fine piece of meat, so I took my chances pan-frying the steak and smothering it with gravy. Every one of us enjoyed the meal, but much later on I learned that's *not* what you do with a good cut of meat.

My father was absent for the occasion.

Uncle Pete came down to Nashville from Stewart County to pick me up. Of all the Wallace children, he lived the closest to his mother, Mamma Pearl, in Big Rock and no doubt felt the most responsible for her well-being. We left straightaway. The eighty-five-mile drive north was quiet. Uncle Pete was a man who had little to say, but when he spoke you listened. His wife had died not that long ago, and he was raising his three kids, my first cousins, on his own. I felt close to him. As we drove, I mentally steeled myself: expect the best, prepare for the worst. The fall colors were just turning.

When we arrived, I felt comforted immediately by memories of having been to the house as a young child—visiting, and also living there for days or weeks at a time when we were homeless. My tight muscles relaxed. As soon as I walked into the house Mamma Pearl embraced me. Like always, she wore a long, faded cotton-print dress that fell to her ankles.

The house stood close to the road at the top of a sharp curve. Mamma Pearl was at one end of the curve and Uncle Pete at the other, within sight of each other, an eighth of a mile apart. Many of Mamma Pearl's family lived nearby—Aunt Marcene two miles north, Uncle Cordell two miles beyond that, and my Great-Aunt Bertha,

Mamma Pearl's sister, lived on a gravel road three miles east, near the house where I'd been born. Along with Potneck and Bumpus Mills, the area of Big Rock was Wallace territory, a labyrinth of blood relations living on land steeped in beautiful rolling hills, rock formations, woods, and creeks—the land of my roots.

Mamma Pearl's house was a small, white two-bedroom clapboard house that had been well maintained by Papa Jim. Off the back porch was a green lawn, Papa Jim's tobacco field, pasture, hog pen, various outbuildings, and beyond all that, the woods.

Trimmed hedges, flowers, and planted grass surrounded the front porch. Inside, Papa Jim and Mamma Pearl had furnished the house with permanent things—rugs, lamps, a sofa, and chairs acquired years before. The living room looked like a well-dusted antique shop. In the front right corner was a small television set and, on a small end table, a telephone. I had never lived in a house with a telephone before.

Off the living room was Mamma Pearl's bedroom. Mine was off the kitchen. The house had electricity, indoor heating, and running water, and the bathroom had a tub. This was the nicest home I had lived in. The only chore assigned to me by Mamma Pearl was to make my bed and keep my room clean. I could do that.

The first night was the hardest. I imagined it must have been difficult for Mamma Pearl as well.

In the evening, I was used to seven other children running around and talking and playing and doing their homework, all within a twelve-by-twelve-foot space. Drama and high-pitched conversation was the general rule. The atmosphere was noisy, rambunctious, and fractious. But at Mamma Pearl's, with just the two of us, except for night sounds of crickets and frogs, there was absolute quiet, so hushed I could hear my footsteps as I walked across the floor. This was lonely backcountry.

That night, before bed, Mamma Pearl sat in her favorite chair in the living room knitting, a ball of yarn settled on her lap. In a low voice, she talked to me about this and that and I got the feeling that she enjoyed having someone to listen to her. She was a woman with a lot to say. As I sat with her, I realized why I was there. Mamma Pearl was an aging woman living on her own on an isolated piece of land. She had family close by, but even though they visited often, they had jobs and children of their own to attend to. Mamma Pearl needed someone to be with her—for companionship and also to be the point person should anything go wrong. I was there to provide those things. I had to accept that I was there for a greater purpose than my own.

As Mamma Pearl knitted, the reality of being back in Stewart County began to sink in. I'd been gone for only two years, but it felt much longer. How was I going to get around with no buses? What was I going to do for money without work? I told Mamma Pearl that I'd forgotten how remote the county was.

"Douglas Wayne, it will be good for you to get reacquainted with your country roots," she said.

The next day, a group of my favorite cousins came over to welcome me back. Three of them were attending Stewart County High School, which was where I was to start that coming Monday. I already knew the high school a little because I'd spent half of my freshman year there before moving to Nashville. Talking with my cousins made me excited to be returning, although I wasn't looking forward to the hour-long school bus ride from Big Rock to Dover, where the county's only high school was situated.

From the first day, things went better than I'd expected. My cousins were there, plus I had forgotten how many kids I knew already from having attended almost all of the various feeder schools. Also, I attained a certain instant popularity having strictly to do with the fact that I had transferred in from a big city, for which Nashville qualified. Any new student who might be bringing in news from the larger world outside Stewart County was showered with attention and a measure of prestige.

I wanted to try out for the basketball team, but practice was strictly after school and I had no transportation home, by public bus or otherwise. Mamma Pearl lived ten miles away from the school. I began to feel stranded and landlocked out at her farm. There wasn't a lot for a teenager to do in Stewart County—the closest movie theater was twenty-five miles away in Clarksville. But even so, other than the woods, there was nowhere I could go unless somebody with a car came by to pick me up. Each time I thought about getting a job to help my circumstances, I knocked my head against the same rock wall: I had no way of getting to a job.

I discussed my dilemma with Mamma Pearl, and she in turn discussed my problem with her sons and daughters. Later in the week, Uncle Pete came by the house and offered to give me a weekly allowance of $2.50. I was grateful and crestfallen at the same time. What was I going to do with $2.50? Not ask a girl out, that's for sure. In my own mind, I felt caught between honoring and dishonoring his generosity. I chose the first.

Uncle Pete called me aside and said, "Now, son, when you're in the store with your buddies and thinking about getting a Coke, be sure not to buy one for everyone else. Spend wisely."

I did.

I was privately grateful for the reminder that if I were going to make it, I would have to make it on my own.

Mamma Pearl and I could always talk, and we talked about almost everything except she didn't like to talk about her snuff addiction. As far as I could tell, that was her only vice. She kept a big pinch of snuff between her lower lip and teeth at all times, and frequently spit into the spittoon she kept next to her chair. To her it wasn't an addiction. Snuff was just something she used to soothe her nerves, she'd tell me, the same way that cigarettes soothe the nerves of smokers.

Mamma Pearl had an unwavering faith in God. I was awed by her commitment to lead a righteous life. She and her sister, my Aunt Bertha, attended church every Sunday morning without fail, and often I went along. Across the gravel road from the church was the graveyard where Papa Jim was buried, and we visited his grave weekly. At home, every now and then, I would catch Mamma Pearl looking at me and she'd say, "You remind me of your Papa Jim," which always filled me with pride. She missed him and I missed him. I also missed my family back in Nashville. I liked writing, so I wrote to them at least once a week. Mamma Pearl supplied the stamps. My letters were primarily directed to my brother Steve, three years younger than me. I begged him to stay in school. As his older brother, I tried to help him deal with the bullies in the neighborhood. He wrote me back and often closed his letters with "Wish you were here" or "I sure could use your help." Mom wrote too. I worried about them. I worried about them not having enough food, especially when Mamma Pearl gave me all the food I could eat.

Sometimes after receiving a letter from home I'd withdraw and wouldn't talk. Mamma Pearl would notice right away. She'd raised four sons and knew exactly how to handle my moodiness. She could disarm me with a certain smile she had. She didn't use it often, but when she did, it was effective. She'd get me drifting onto another track by saying things like, "Douglas Wayne, you're going to make some girl a very happy wife someday." At times like that I'd believe it was a gift from God that I'd been sent to live with her.

One night in the living room, Mamma Pearl asked me what I wanted to do after graduating from high school. I told her that I was going to go to college. She looked at me kindly. "Well, there is many a slip twixt the cup and the lip," she said.

I was sitting on the floor by her favorite chair. She was doing her evening knitting. We both fell silent.

I let her words sink in. I knew her well enough to know she wasn't trying to throw cold water on my dream. But my grandmother never pulled any punches when it came to facing hard truths. Know that there will be challenges, she was trying to say. Move forward, but proceed with blinders *off*. Be aware that the road will be particularly difficult for you. Many things can and will happen between now and an admission to college.

Mamma Pearl understood what it was going to take and that touched me.

Expect the best, prepare for the worst.

My grades at Stewart County High were mostly A's. College was going to mean writing a slew of essays, I knew, so I decided to enroll in the school's typing class, which was 90 percent girls. That suited me fine. We practiced on manual typewriters, the ones that sound a bell at the end of every line to let you know it's time to return the carriage. I was surprised to find the sounds of all of us typing at once soothing, the clacking of the keys, the dings of the bells, and the thumps of the carriage returns—all at different speeds, in different rhythms. That and the scenery of the pretty girls typing made the time pass quickly. As it turned out, I had a natural talent for typing. I had no idea how useful this skill would later prove to be.

As far as girls were concerned, if I wanted my arm around some-one, there was always a girl who wanted to be embraced. There was always a girl interested in me and there was always a girl I was inter-ested in, and sometimes those interests were mutual. Getting a date wasn't a problem, but not having a car, as many of my classmates did, *was* a problem. Mamma Pearl's house was miles away from the girls I wanted to spend more time with and who wanted to spend time with me. But who knows what kind of trouble I would have gotten myself into if I'd had an automobile.

CHAPTER TWENTY-TWO

A Game of Chicken

In June 1966, after I finished my junior year, the Wallace family agreed on my return to Nashville for the summer. I didn't like leaving Mamma Pearl alone, but I needed to make money for college. She understood. I'd be away only until the fall, when I'd go back to Stewart County for my senior year.

I came home to find my family's living conditions deteriorated. From Trinity Lane, already a poor neighborhood, they had moved to 802 South Seventh Street in a massive government housing project about four miles away. This was the last stop before a fall into home-lessness. Bracy refused to live in the projects and had started staying with my mother's brother, our Uncle Virgil. Faye had married while I was away and lived with her husband, Wally, whose mother owned a bar on Gallatin Road. Faye continued to take care of Tim and Brady during the day, because Mom was still working at Field Crutcher for minimum wage.

When I opened the front screen-door, torn and bellied out, Mom was in the kitchen cooking. Her face shone with joy when she turned and saw me. The nine months I'd been away evaporated. My father was home, too, and his lifeless eyes and slack body said all I needed to know. Greeting him was awkward, cold, at arm's length.

Later, when we were alone, I asked Mom if he was still abusing her.

"He knows better than to hit me," she said. "I'll call the police."

But her response wasn't convincing. I considered confronting him, but practiced restraint. I was going to be home for three months. I figured my presence provided a measure of protection for my mother. If I went at it with him, neither of us could continue living under the same roof. And he wouldn't be the one to leave.

The apartment was too small for the family, even with two fewer children. The interior walls were concrete block. The walls, floors, and ceilings of each room were painted light gray. It was like a warren of jail cells. In the living room were a secondhand couch, two used chairs, and a resurrected black-and-white television, which sat on a small table by the front door. The kitchen had just enough room for a stove, a sink, and a refrigerator, all of these in deplorable condition. We took turns eating on a bare metal table with four chairs. On the wall hung a flyswatter for the flies, mosquitoes, and roaches—the same extermination method we'd used on Trinity Lane. Upstairs was a pitiful bathroom and three tiny, boxlike bedrooms.

The housing projects themselves stretched several blocks, in rows of two-story, red-brick buildings, one after another, all alike. Our apartment was a center unit in one of these featureless buildings. Sharing a front stoop with the people next door, it faced an identical row of drab apartments directly across a narrow strip of lawn, more dirt than grass. The grounds and alleyways were dirty and dangerous, strewn with broken glass and empty bottles and the desperate discards of people at the bottom. Rats frequented the dumpsters. I was reminded of the ugliness of the Granite City projects ten years before, only these in East Nashville were worse. Crowded conditions and lack of privacy induced a chronic, seething irritation and edgy relationships between residents. Arguments and shouting across the courtyards were standard fare, especially in the steam-heat of summer.

My younger brothers Steve and Rick had warned me about the violence on South Seventh Street, and they were right. What I saw in my first week made the aggression on Trinity Lane look tame by comparison. Walking any of the streets in the housing projects involved considerable risk. But South Seventh, where we were, had acquired a hard-core, outlaw reputation all its own. You could read it in the slashes of graffiti that covered every surface. You could hear it in the angry voices behind torn curtains billowing in open windows. You could feel the volcanic tension walking by a group of restive males. Almost everyone I would come to know, some as young as eight, carried a weapon—a knife, brass knuckles, a gun. The projects were a breeding ground for criminal behavior and also drug and alcohol addiction.

This place scared me, but I had no choice but to adapt, to cope with it. Like a young cat arriving in a new home, I traversed the neighborhood stealthily, zigzagging down alleyways to get to the bus stop three blocks away on Shelby Avenue. I scoped out the territory with deliberate caution, getting familiar with it, finding my way. Violence in the projects was 24-7. There were no days off. Every resident, and there were thousands, was either engaging in it, observing it, talking about it, or cowering from it. There was no escaping the reality that, eventually, I would become a victim of it.

One of my first chance encounters—and they were all chance encounters—occurred on the project grounds when I was spotted by a group of five tough-looking boys, about my age, who started walking toward me. To show no fear, I didn't alter my pace. They were friendly, in a rough sort of way, and asked if I wanted to hang out with them. I didn't want to get any closer to these guys but, again, to show no fear, I followed them to a vacant apartment with broken windows and a busted door. After we slipped inside, they each pulled knives out of their pockets and asked if I knew how to play chicken. I said no. So they showed me. One of the boys stood flat against a wall with his legs about shoulder-distance apart, his arms akimbo. From ten feet away, the other four then took turns throwing their knives in his direction, aiming as accurately as possible to see who could stick his knife closest to the guy standing against the wall—without harming him. When offered a knife, I declined, saying that I wasn't comfortable with my accuracy, which I wasn't and which they accepted. Eventually, my turn came to stand at the wall. I was scared to death. I felt certain it was a setup to stick a knife in my gut. One at a time, four knives came at me, one coming close to my face, another between my legs. I didn't flinch. Not on the outside. On South Seventh Street a person had to prove his mettle. By not flinching I was given the respect accorded to those who know the code of the neighborhood—never show fear. But it would be a mistake to consider these guys friends. They traveled in a group of five, presumably out of fear and to ensure their own safety. Their efforts to bully me with the game of chicken told me all I needed to know about these guys. I didn't trust a single one of them.

Far from the neighborhood, I found a full-time, white-collar summer job at a title insurance company in downtown Nashville. My job was to conduct title searches to ensure that a property could be transferred to a potential buyer free and clear of all liens or judgments. The company trained me in this research, which involved plowing through property records stored in dozens of fat, hardbound books kept in the record room of the county courthouse, where I spent the larger part of my workday. The job didn't pay well, but the research was technical and related to the legal profession, so I was thrilled. For the first time, I was required to wear a shirt and tie to work.

One day at the courthouse on Union Street a man wearing a dark gray suit, light blue shirt, and matching tie walked into the record room as if he owned the place. His black shoes shone and he had thick, gray hair that was combed back neatly and fanned slightly over the top of his ears. He had the polished look of a lawyer, and I admired his confident swagger.

Working next to me was another researcher doing title searches for a competing title company. We'd become friends. In a low voice, he said to me, out of nowhere, "Don't say anything bad about the Democratic Party."

"Who cares about the Democratic Party?" I said, perplexed, in a normal tone of voice and, as it happened, within earshot of the well-dressed, gray-haired man, who suddenly turned in my direction.

"That's the County Commissioner," my friend whispered. "He's one of the biggest Democrats around."

The man signaled to the records clerk and the two of them disappeared into a private room. I thought nothing more about it for the rest of the afternoon, completed my title searches, and walked back to the company office, where my boss motioned me to his office as I came through the front entrance.

He told me that there had been a complaint about me. The County Commissioner had called. The commissioner had told my manager that he never wanted to see my face in the courthouse again. The manager then explained that Tennessee Title couldn't afford enemies in the courthouse. I was terminated on the spot.

Up to this time, I'd had no experience with politics. I made a mental note to avoid politicians in the future. I had no choice but to get over the sting of being fired. Until I found another job, though, I had the opportunity to do other things, like spending time with my brother Bracy, who'd decided to enlist in the U.S. Air Force and was awaiting word.

Bracy had taken up drinking after our move to Nashville, when we were still living on Trinity Lane. In fact, it was Bracy who introduced me to alcohol at that time. I got drunk on a few occasions, but then made the conscious decision to back off from booze, from drinking for the sake of getting drunk. I feared alcohol. The last man I wanted to bear any resemblance to was my alcoholic father.

As the oldest and the son of a drunk, I think Bracy was motivated by a strong sense of duty to help support the family. My father did nothing to discourage Bracy—a good student—from dropping out of high school. If anything, he told Bracy he was doing a good thing. By putting Bracy to work full-time, my father was taking the load off his own shoulders.

Bracy wasn't violent when he drank; he didn't drive while intoxicated, and he restricted his heavy drinking to weekends. However, prone to bad hangovers, he often failed to show up for work on Monday mornings. Like my father, he started having a problem holding on to a steady job. It broke my heart to see this. Of my five brothers, I was closest to Bracy. He was one of the kindest members of the family. He was seventeen when we moved to Nashville, and especially vulnerable to outside influences. Crushing poverty and a despicable father had drained his confidence. I feared that Bracy's dreams for a stake in the future were slipping away. Dropping out of high school had left him with few resources to overcome the challenges posed by his environment, another victim of generational poverty.

CHAPTER TWENTY-THREE

Crime Doesn't Pay

One midsummer day, Bracy suggested we take a ride to Dover. He knew that I was good friends with several of the girls from Stewart County High School and wanted me to set him up with a date. We took his black 1953 Ford sedan, V-8 engine. He loved that car, and had done a lot of work on it. We met the girls, spent the afternoon and evening with them in Dover, and then headed straight back home, stopping at a gas station past Clarksville at around eleven o'clock.

After Bracy asked the gas station attendant to fill up the tank, he leaned over to me sitting in the passenger seat and whispered, "I'm taking off as soon as he finishes filling up the car." I couldn't tell if he was joking. It was completely out of character if he wasn't. We hadn't discussed it beforehand, nor to my knowledge had Bracy ever done anything like this before. The sly smile on his face could have meant anything.

The attendant had just screwed the gas cap back on when Bracy made his move. He popped the clutch and the car bolted forward, with tires squealing, as we shot out of the gas station and onto the empty, nighttime highway. In seconds, it seemed, we reached a hundred miles an hour and then accelerated to a speed which the speedometer couldn't register. In shock, I looked back to see if anyone was following us. In the distance I saw faint headlights fast approaching. "He's coming after us," I said.

"I see him," Bracy said calmly, seemingly unfazed.

Dead silence and total concentration took over as we continued to fly down a long stretch of highway. Unblinking, I stared straight ahead. Suddenly, I heard in front of us the unmistakable sound of crushing metal. The car window had gone completely black. I couldn't see a thing. Then I realized that the hood had become unhinged and thrown back against the windshield by the thrust of our speed. Bracy wasn't even close to slowing down.

I stole a quick glance at him. To my astonishment, he was driving the car with his head stuck out of the driver's window. He wasn't giving in. Indeed, he seemed to be enjoying the chase. Next, I thought for sure we were going to crash when I heard the engine throw a rod and instantly smelled oil coming from the blown engine. Now there was no choice. Bracy let the car roll to a gentle stop on the side of the road.

Flashing its headlights, the chasing car came upon us from behind. The driver introduced himself as the proprietor of the gas station. He told us to stay in the car and that the sheriff had been called and was on his way. Moments later, the whirling red lights of the county sheriff's vehicle announced his arrival.

The sheriff took us both to the Cheatham County Jail, where we spent a sleepless night on a cold, concrete slab. The next morning the sheriff told us that the owner had felt sorry for us and dropped all charges. We were free to go. I was relieved, embarrassed, and sorry. We had to hitchhike back to Nashville. The Ford had been totaled and Bracy never went back to reclaim it. He'd driven his car to death, losing his prized possession for ten dollars' worth of gas.

For me, it was a stark lesson: Crime doesn't pay.

Bracy, however, didn't learn a thing. Lack of money can bring about poor choices. Just days after he'd replaced the Ford with a beat-up 1958 Chevrolet Impala, the need for gasoline led him to a similar impulsive action. The two of us were riding around East Nashville on a Friday night, when Bracy pulled into a dark alley and parked.

"I'm going to get some gas," he said.

"You remember the last time we did this, Bracy?" I said.

"Don't worry. Watch out for me and honk the horn if you see anything."

I remained in the car and watched Bracy take an empty, five-gallon gas can out of the trunk and then walk across the alley to a dimly lit, partially filled parking lot, where I lost sight of him. A few minutes later, carrying an obviously now-full gas container, he came running toward the car. He jumped into the driver's seat and took off, with no one chasing after us this time.

Near the housing projects, we stopped at a convenience store. Bracy poured the gasoline into the tank, and we bought some Cokes. We resumed driving and, just as we slowed down for a speed bump, a police cruiser traveling in the opposite direction passed us. The patrol officers took a long look at us and I could tell from their flinty eyes that we were going to get pulled over. Sure enough, the cruiser made a flip-turn. Slowing quickly to a stop, Bracy told me to get out and start walking, which I did. The police cruiser then came up behind Bracy and signaled him to pull over. At the same time, another police car pulled up alongside me and ordered me into the backseat. I'd been walking in plain sight, pretending to be a disinterested pedestrian. Apparently, the night watchman had witnessed Bracy siphoning the gasoline and had reported it to the police, along with a description of the vehicle. The just-emptied container in the trunk was all the evidence necessary for an arrest.

We were both taken to the Davidson County Metropolitan Jail in downtown Nashville. Because he was twenty, Bracy was booked as an adult and released several hours later on a fifty-dollar bond. Under eighteen, I was transferred to a juvenile facility a few miles away, where I was assigned a single cell with a short metal cot and no lights. I couldn't see my hands in front of my face. I was being treated like a criminal and I felt like one.

The next morning, breakfast came on a tray through a slot in the solid metal door that only opened from the outside. The twelve-by-twelve-inch window was covered with a metal plate so the light was dim. Soon after, a guard, not in the mood for conversation, opened my cell door and pointed me in the direction of the detention lounge—a large, open, windowless room with a television suspended from the ceiling and folding chairs scattered around the room. Bright fluorescent ceiling lights reflected off the grayish-white linoleum floors. I looked around the room and chose a corner spot with nothing to obstruct my view. I sat down, propping up my feet on a vacant chair.

The room slowly filled up as more inmates were released from their cells, the majority looking sixteen or seventeen. Suddenly, poised for a fight, a tall, muscular guy with a scar beneath his left eye walked up to me and kicked the chair out from under my feet. I jumped up and got into a shoving match with him, which immediately escalated to a fistfight. Other inmates stepped in and broke it up before the guard showed. We both walked away, each of us willing to let the conflict end.

I spent the weekend at this facility and watched the pattern repeat itself. One of the inmates would start a fight when the guard was out of the room and then others would break it up just before the guard returned. Just like the schoolyard, an ugly pecking order had been established in the juvenile detention lounge—the strongest fighters occupied the top and those unable or unwilling to defend themselves, the bottom. It was the inescapable initiation for every new inmate. To guarantee their safety, the weaker guys were also intimidated into paying money to veteran inmates. But paying protection money didn't mean being treated with respect. The choices were fight, and fight well, or lose any semblance of dignity.

Because I'd fought back on Saturday morning, I was able to spend the rest of the weekend in jail without further incident and was released to Mom on Monday. My court date was scheduled in a month's time.

A criminal record, even juvenile, could ruin my chances of becoming a lawyer. I was acutely aware of this—and worried. According to the statutes, I was guilty. Even though I hadn't been the person committing the crime, I'd had an obligation either to leave the crime scene before the crime was committed, or to stop the crime from happening. The law was unambiguous.

CHAPTER TWENTY-FOUR

Out of My League

I had turned seventeen in July. By this time I felt as if I were slowly being swallowed up by the violence in the housing projects. The tension of living there was unrelenting. My determination to work helped. After Tennessee Title, I went back to parking cars for the owner of several downtown lots, where I'd worked the summer before. The owner, Jack, was a silver-haired man in his sixties, who drove long-haul trips for Greyhound, and he'd remembered me. The job kept me busy and I enjoyed building friendly relationships with the regular customers and, especially, the big tippers. Those who tipped well, when heading out, could expect to find their car up front, ready for immediate departure, the air-conditioning running. The lot's manager, Jim, was a twenty-eight-year-old schoolteacher who'd been working for Jack every summer since he was my age. At the close of each business day, he made sure all the money was properly accounted for. He was a real straight arrow, the opposite of what I encountered every day in the projects. The people in the projects were unlike any people I had ever known or even knew existed. Before the summer ended, I experienced a number of close calls.

One hot afternoon, I was walking through the open field behind the projects' half-ruined community center when I heard a screaming altercation coming from outside one of the housing units. About seventy-five feet away, I saw a teenage boy, about sixteen, arguing with a woman, probably his mother. The woman spotted me looking in their direction and shouted, "Mind your own business!"

I stopped, unsure whether she was speaking to me.

"Yeah, I'm talking to you!" she said.

I turned away, ignoring her, but from the corner of my eye saw the boy coming toward me. Stopping three feet in front of me, he said, "What did you say to my mother?"

"I didn't say anything," I replied.

I could tell by his eyes that he wanted a fight, so when he attempted a sucker punch to my face, I was prepared. I blocked the punch easily and hit him with a right cross. Blood gushed from his nose.

"You broke my nose!" he screamed, clutching both hands over his face.

His mother ran over and grabbed her son, cursing at me and yelling obscenities.

"You m—. You broke my son's nose!"

"I didn't start the fight," I shot back.

"I know where you live, punk," she said. "You come back here at five-thirty and give my boy a chance to settle this or we're coming to your place." Her gnarled face and biting tongue told me she meant business. I started for home.

"Don't make me knock on your door!" she shouted after me.

A neighborhood friend who'd come outside to see what the shouting was about warned me that the woman was a lunatic. "She's out-of-her-mind crazy," he said.

For the next couple of hours at home, all I could think about was the real possibility that this crazy lady would come knocking at 5:30.

I couldn't allow this unpredictable, volatile woman near my family. I saw no way out, so I decided to show up at the appointed place. I arrived early and hid behind a hedge with a good view of the boy's front door. If he showed up without his mother, I was going to settle things the usual way. But I had a bad feeling.

At 5:20, the boy walked out of his apartment with his mother close behind. His face was bandaged heavily around the nose. He appeared nervous and was obviously having words with his mother, who took a seat on the front stoop and motioned him toward the community center. I kept my eye on the mother until I was certain she was not going to follow.

The boy appeared to be holding no weapons. As he approached, I stepped out from behind the hedge and faced him. Startled, he took a step back. He looked toward his mother and yelled, "Mom, here he is!"

She started running in our direction. Then I saw her reach her hand into her purse. A wave of chills rushed through me. I'd never been up against a gun before. I turned and ran and heard the rapid fire of gunshots coming from behind me. Bullets struck the community center. I ran across the street toward the back of our apartment and then around to the front courtyard where a small group of residents had quickly gathered at the sound of gunfire. I rushed to safety in the middle of this crowd and waited. But the woman didn't pursue me into my own piece of the projects.

The police were called and the mother arrested. They interviewed me, took a statement, and told me I'd be called as a witness. But that was the last I ever heard of the woman or her son.

It was a mistake to try to get comfortable in this neighborhood. I could deal with fistfights, but not a gun. The violence on South Seventh Street was completely out of my league. During the next few weeks, for protective camouflage, I actively began seeking out friends from the projects. They were all tough guys to varying degrees, and I knew getting closer carried risks. But it was safer to hang out with them than to walk the streets alone. Traveling in groups, you were less likely to be confronted, except perhaps by those within your own group. Even then, the general rule was that no one pulled a knife or a gun against a member of the group. I ended up purchasing a yellow-handled, banana-shaped knife that I practiced with until, using a one-handed flick, I could open it faster than someone using a switchblade. The technique was called "knife-flipping." Kids under ten knew how to flip knives; old men and women knew how to flip knives. It wasn't a game, but a matter of survival. I had no intention of using my knife as a weapon, and never did so. It was an effective prop. I was far safer on South Seventh Street because I owned a knife than I would have been without one. Outwardly, like an actor playing a role, I acted like a tough street kid, but inside I was a scared person desperately wanting out of the environment.

One Friday night, as I was walking to the local store, one of my new friends from the projects, Danny Johnson, pulled up to the curb in a sweet, dark blue Ford Falcon with fender skirts and lots of chrome.

"Want to hang out?" he asked.

"Do I get the shotgun seat?" I said.

A cute, blonde girl quickly jumped out of the passenger seat and joined Danny's friend, Bill, in the backseat. Bill's face was pitted and you could tell his nose had been broken at least once.

"It's all yours," she said.

The girl's name was Karen. Like most girls in the housing projects, she had a street-tough appearance that most outsiders would call "white trash." She did a lot of loud trash-talking. I'd heard that she'd been in and out of juvenile detention.

For the next couple of hours we cruised around our section of East Nashville, stopping occasionally to talk with other kids. Danny had a reputation as a fighter and had been known to use a knife, but he also liked to have fun and he'd given me no reason not to trust him. But anytime you accept a ride in East Nashville, you have to be aware that you're accepting a measure of risk.

The night had been going very well. We were all having a great time. Around ten o'clock, Danny stopped for gas. While the gas station attendant was filling the tank, the four of us filled the inside of the car with random, easy talk. Suddenly, Karen pulled a small handgun out of her purse.

Smiling coyly, she said, "We're going to rob this place."

Her manner was calm and matter-of-fact. Clearly, she'd come to this decision on her own. And I wanted no part of it. Because of my experience with Bracy, I knew without a doubt that, were she to go through with it, every passenger in the vehicle would be guilty of felony robbery, whether or not he participated, whether or not he approved.

Without thinking about the consequences, I slapped Karen across the side of her face, at the same time snatching the gun from her hand.

"You're not robbing anyone as long as I'm in this car," I said.

The car fell into absolute quiet. Danny, Bill, and Karen stared at me. Danny paid the tab.

"Take me home right now," I demanded. "You guys can rob whoever you want after I am out of this car. Until then, I'm keeping the gun." As Danny headed toward my apartment, which was ten minutes away, I emptied the bullets from the twenty-two, but held on to the pistol.

Karen then snapped out of her shock and flew into a molten rage. "I'll kill you!" she said. I was no stranger to rage. I prayed that I would get home before things went completely out of control.

I considered asking Danny to stop the car and let me out right there, but I knew it might be interpreted as a sign of weakness and showing weakness in the housing projects was never good, even to guys who were supposed to be your friends.

"No man hits me and gets away with it," Karen screamed.

Her comment all of a sudden reminded me of Mom being hit by Dad. It pierced me through and I felt ashamed.

"You're not getting away with this," she said, pounding her strong fists against the back of my seat.

I turned to her and said levelly, "You don't want to mess with me." Then I placed the unloaded pistol in her open palm. Our eyes were locked, neither one of us showing fear. In that moment, she could have used the gun as a weapon of blunt force. Instead, she put the pistol into her purse, never once taking her eyes away from mine. We stayed looking at each other until Danny pulled up in front of my complex. After stepping out of the car, I said to Karen through the back window, "I promise you that I have never hit a girl before this day and I'll never do it again, ever. I'm so sorry."

As I walked away, I wondered if she would reload the gun and shoot me in the back.

I heard the car door open and, when I turned to look, it was Karen moving up to the shotgun seat. She gave me a faint smile that hinted at forgiveness—or maybe future revenge. I couldn't tell for sure.

After that night, I avoided riding in cars with people from the neighborhood. But one last perilous encounter awaited me.

CHAPTER TWENTY-FIVE

An Encounter with an Outlaw

I n early August, I was out one night with Bobby Sims, a friend— a safe friend—who lived in the projects a few blocks away from me. Bobby was street-savvy but not street-tough. He wasn't a skilled fighter, losing more than he won. In a way, he looked to me for protection. It was just after dark, but the air was still hot and close. Bobby and I had walked over to the store to get something cold to drink. Bobby grabbed a soda and I purchased a Coke and a small bag of peanuts. As a young boy, I'd learned that a Coca-Cola tastes better when you pour salted peanuts into the bottle. Thereafter, I always drank my Coke with peanuts.

As we exited the store, three older guys were walking in. We stepped aside to let them pass, and I thought I recognized one of them. "Hi, John," I said.

The guy looked at me point-blank, and that's when I knew he was the wrong man at the wrong time, and that I was in trouble. The John I knew was an ex-con trying to turn his life around. This hard-faced, heavy-lidded man wasn't anyone I knew. His skin looked like the leather of rhinoceros hide—tough. Under dark eyebrows, his eyes narrowed.

"Why did you call me John?" he demanded angrily.

"I'm sorry," I said. "I thought you were someone else."

He moved closer. He was about my height, six feet, and his stance was rigid. I stepped backward, but bumped into the side of a parked car behind me, which caught me momentarily off-guard. Before I could react, he struck me with a powerful uppercut beneath my chin, which lifted me off the ground and over the hood of the car. I rolled off on the other side and landed solidly on all fours. I jumped to my feet and saw the guy running toward me, on a mission to inflict further damage. I don't think he was expecting the punch I landed across the left side of his face. He ran straight into it, falling backward to the ground. When I heard his head hit the asphalt, I thought the punch had been a knockout blow.

"What do you think I should do with this guy?" I asked Bobby, who was standing by, wide-eyed and anxious. My anger was intense. I considered a swift kick to his face or stomach, slamming my knees against his shoulder, and other terrible things. I was looking to Bobby to cool me down.

"Look out!" Bobby said.

I turned just in time to see the guy take a stabbing lunge at me with a hawk-blade knife, a deadly weapon designed to inflict maximum damage by ripping through the skin and muscle. The tip of the knife blade curves inward, like the beak of a hawk, thus the name "hawk-blade."

The knife entered on the left side of my chest, slicing deep into my pectorals. I tried defending myself, but another swing of the knife cut deep into the flesh of my right wrist. I knew that if I didn't get away he was going to kill me. His attack was relentless. I was carrying my knife, but had vowed never to use it in a fight. I grappled for a way to run without getting stabbed in the back. I jumped back just in time to avoid another stabbing, and that's when I took off.

The attacker gave chase but I managed to outrun him. I checked into the emergency room of a local hospital to get the wounds treated and stitched and was back on the street about two hours later. Bobby had stayed with me. Coming home that night I was seriously concerned that I might not survive the last few weeks of summer.

The following Monday morning, I showed up for work at the parking lot with a noticeable bandage on my right wrist.

"What happened to your wrist?" the manager, Jim, asked me.

"Some guy jumped me."

I noticed that blood had seeped through the bandage. Slightly embarrassed, I covered it with my left hand. Jim seemed genuinely concerned and wanted to know the details. When I finished the story, he said, "You've got to learn a better way to survive over there or they will kill you."

He stepped out and came back with a first-aid kit, which he used to clean and dress my wound. He said we would discuss this further when he returned that evening to balance the books. I was planning on working the evening shift.

During the day, my wrist continued to bleed. I needed my right hand to drive, which meant tearing the stitches. By the time Jim came back, my bandage was a bloody mess.

"You okay?" he asked.

"Yeah."

"You look worse."

He redressed the wound with a fresh bandage and gave me a ride home. After that day, Jim became my mentor, spending hours teaching me how to fight and defend myself, especially against knife attacks. I hadn't known that Jim was a fighter. For the rest of the summer, the parking lot was our boxing school. Jim coached me in mastering the art of slap-boxing, a fighting strategy he had perfected. To slap-box is to strike a hard, lightning-fast slap to an opponent's face, which throws him off-guard and allows you to control the fight. Once you master the slap, there is no defense and you can alternatively switch from slap-boxing to hard punches. As a fighting strategy, what I liked most about it was that I didn't necessarily have to hurt my opponent to win. I learned how to use my quick hands to punish my opponent so rapidly, five or six slaps in fleet succession, so the fight was over within seconds, and no one really got hurt.

Jim and I shared a philosophy: Never start a fight—always finish it.

Soon after the knife attack, I learned that my attacker was a well-known criminal from the projects named Jesse Outlaw. "Outlaw" may sound like a street name, but in this case, it was his actual surname and one common in Tennessee. I went to school with several Outlaws in Stewart County, and there were many in Nashville. He'd been in and out of jail since childhood, and had hurt a lot of people. He had the reputation of a ruthless felon with no regard for human life.

The following year I heard that Jesse Outlaw had been killed while serving time in the Davidson County Jail. I imagined that he had gotten into a fight with someone just as heartless as he was.

Now, I consider it a blessing that I was the one who got hurt that night. If I had won that fight, Mr. Outlaw would not have stood for the humiliation of a public beating. He would have hunted me down and shot me in the back or fatally knifed me.

Not long after that fight, I received an invitation to dinner from Jack, the parking lot owner, and his wife. They lived in a big, beautiful colonial house near Vanderbilt University. After we ate, Jack and I went into his study and talked. He told me that he and his wife spoke of me often, admired my character, and wanted to help me achieve my lifetime goals. He asked me if I would consider moving into their home and becoming part of their family—they had no children of their own. He and his wife were in their sixties.

He went into detail about helping to pay my expenses for college and law school, and providing money for clothing and a new car.

As I listened to him, I was stunned. He was talking about eventual adoption, which seemed outrageous to me. I knew that Jack and his wife had taken a genuine interest in me, but I was totally unprepared for this discussion. There wasn't the slightest possibility that I would accept his offer, which I told him explicitly. I said that he'd offended me and my family and that I was "not for sale." I asked him to give me a ride home immediately. My instant reaction was fury.

In the car, he apologized profusely and seemed upset and uncomfortable that his offer had created a problem between us. Later, I regretted that my response had been so emotional, so angry, and so instantaneous. I believe the initial trigger had to do with my close bond with my mother and my family. Family was first for me. I reacted to the idea of being separated from them. Then the offer of material help set off a chain reaction. I exploded because Jack's offer made me feel small. His offer threatened to diminish my perception of my own competence. There's a mindset to being poor that I've observed to be practically impossible for the nonpoor to penetrate. That mindset has an axiomatic logic all its own. It makes you resentful when someone better off than you offers help. In my case, I perceived offers of help as insults . . . Did Jack mean that only an outsider could help me? Was he saying that I couldn't help myself?

Absent the anger and the mindset, I might have said to him, "Your offer is very generous and I thank you, but I'd rather make it on my own," or "Thank you, but no."

Near the end of summer Bracy was accepted into the air force. Enlisting in the military, I think, was his way of trying to create a plan for his life. He hoped to get his GED and then go to college on the GI Bill. However, I also knew that joining the air force was an afterthought for Bracy, an idea to avoid criminal prosecution for the gasoline theft. Four years in the military during wartime is a long tour of duty. I was worried that my brother had made a life-altering decision on the spur of the moment. I was concerned for his safety and for his future. Bracy was one of the most fun-loving people I knew, but he was also impulsive and incautious, and I was worried that his behavior was going to get him in trouble with the law again.

After learning that Bracy had joined the air force, the court dropped all charges against him for the gasoline theft in East Nashville. I was also fortunate. At my hearing, the juvenile court judge let me off with a stern warning: "I'm giving you a break. Next time, you won't get off so easily." In the juvenile court system, a judge has full discretion. He can issue a sentence, which goes on the record, or he can drop the charges, which happened in my case. This was my first offense, which is what got me off. I promised myself that there was never going to be a "next time." I already had enough obstacles standing between me and becoming a lawyer without having a criminal record.

The summer had shaken me. It had been the worst summer of my life so far. The three months in the projects had gotten under my skin and undermined my confidence in any sort of future free of abject poverty and in-your-face violence. I was having doubts about myself and my abilities to persevere and overcome. I think there were many times during my childhood that I experienced depression, but I started to feel like I was living in hell. I remember being told while studying the Civil War in school that General Sherman had said, "War is hell." South Seventh Street was like that—a war zone. Living there was like living in hell. Living with my father only made it worse.

For the first time, I felt anger and resentment at there being no easy solutions for me, at having to be solely accountable for how my life was going to turn out. The high road seemed far too hard. Yet I'd seen firsthand what happens to a life when you give up and start living on entitlements, start *feeling* entitled, expecting generous handouts to compensate for the hardships. Everything dead-ends. Your strengths atrophy.

During the horrors of World War II, Winston Churchill said, "If you are going through hell, keep going." I believe what kept me seeking an honorable road, even in despair, even with the fatigue of trying so hard to survive, was my connection to my higher power, my candle in the dark, however dim the flame. No matter where I was, emotionally or geographically, I could tap into the profound solace of that light and know that everything was going to be all right, that I was all right, at the core.

CHAPTER TWENTY-SIX

"As the Old Fella Says"

With the summer over, the time had come to return to Mamma Pearl's in Big Rock. It was hard saying good-bye to my family, but I couldn't wait to distance myself from South Seventh Street. Staring out the car window, I may have been shell-shocked, but I wasn't thinking about thugs. I was looking at the trees and wondering if the leaves were going to change early this fall.

Seeing Mamma Pearl again was swell. She looked the same. I felt as if I'd grown another skin since I'd last seen her. But, once again, I felt immediately comforted by the beauty of Stewart County, the lushness of its greenery, the flowing creeks, the near absence of asphalt.

But things were different now. Though I was safe here, I knew it was only a temporary respite. My head ached from trying to figure out how I was going to pay my own way through college, assuming that I qualified in the first place.

Soon after returning, I spoke one night to my grandmother about my college concerns. She was sitting in her usual chair, surrounded by her Bible, her knitting, a can of snuff, the small spittoon. The chair was positioned near the front door, which she kept open to allow cool breezes to enter the house.

"Mamma Pearl, do you think I'll make it to college?" I asked. In retrospect, I realize I was seeking reassurance.

She stopped her knitting and kept her eyes focused on the colorful wool scarf she had been working on. I could always tell when my grandmother was thinking hard about something. She had a nervous habit of using her three middle fingers to caress the skin between her upper lip and nose.

"Douglas Wayne," she finally said. "The good Lord never burdens us with more than we can bear."

Mamma Pearl was raised in Stewart County at a time when children rarely completed middle school and only rich folks attended college. Her cool, impersonal delivery suggested to me that she had failed to grasp the urgency of my college concerns. I wanted to interrogate her, to debate her if necessary, but her response was clearly her final word on the matter.

Shortly thereafter, my great-aunt Bertha came over to visit with Mamma Pearl. Listening to the two sisters talking would confuse most people, but I had learned to understand their language. They often spoke at the same time, but heard fully what the other was saying. They had the peculiar habit of occasionally launching a sentence with the words, "As the old fella says," usually for the purpose of driving home a point. For example, if one of them wanted to end a train of conversation, she might have said something like, "As the old fella says, I think it is better to leave that subject for another day."

The previous summer, before I had grown accustomed to their idiosyncratic ways of talking, I'd been curious about this guy and who he was. I thought perhaps he had been an old friend who'd died.

"Who's the old fella?" I asked them one day.

They both fell silent for a moment and I could tell from the sober expressions on their faces that they were each giving the question serious consideration.

Finally, Aunt Bertha said, "Well, he's the old fella."

And they resumed their conversation, a hint of a smile on Mamma Pearl's face.

On the Saturday that Aunt Bertha visited, she asked me about Nashville. "Douglas Wayne, did you enjoy your summer vacation?" Such a direct question from her to me was rare. Hearing her refer to my summer on South Seventh Street as a vacation was almost hilarious. But since coming back, I'd wanted to tell someone about all the things that had happened—and about living in a world turned upside down, where carrying a knife is a good thing. I was even willing to tell on myself about going to jail. With a potentially understanding ear so close, I was practically bursting.

"Well, Aunt Bertha, let's just say that things didn't turn out the way I had expected," I said.

In most circumstances, this would whet the listener's curiosity and the next logical step in the dialogue would be the question, "What happened?"

Not for Aunt Bertha, who instead said, "Well, Douglas Wayne, as the old fella says, you cannot question the ways of the Lord."

"Surreal" best describes my first day back at school. Returning to Stewart County High School was like being dropped into a foreign country. I couldn't shake the soiled feeling left over from the summer. I felt like a soldier coming back from a war that nobody knows about. And even though I had managed to buy new, clean, stylish clothes for the start of my senior year, I felt like the dirty laundry of poverty would never leave me.

The first morning, waiting for the bell to ring, I stood in the hallway watching the kids divide up into the usual groups: the popular kids, the misfits, the nerds, and the tough guys. I tended to move in and out of these groups as I pleased. This first day, I found myself lingering around with a group of guys I knew in the popular crowd. Our conversation focused on girls and flirtatious glances darted back and forth across the hall. The Presley look, which had held on through the early sixties, was out; guys were now wearing their hair longer and their pants tighter, including me. I noticed the latest "hip" slang and it was as if while I was away for the summer somebody had changed the definition of cool. The whole scene was becoming a "bummer" for me, but it was "out of sight" to be noticed by the "fox" who was "decked out" in a "boss" outfit. Listening to some "cat" talk about "scoring" with this "far-out chick" was a real "drag." I had the urge to say "flake off," as I was "hacked" and wanted to "book." We didn't talk like that in the projects.

I was doing my best to pass as a typical, college-bound senior on his first day of class, though I felt desperate inside. I felt further set apart listening to the guys talk about their fun summers. I couldn't help but wonder what they'd think about mine.

One day early in the term, Mr. Craig, the high school coach, came over to me and said, "You don't want to be like those people you're hanging around with." He was referring to the popular kids. I didn't know the nature of his criticism, but I remember thinking, *I only wish I were like them, I only wish I had their lives.*

Coach Craig seemed to take an interest in me, and he was one of the few teachers who actually talked to students in a real way. The year before, he approached me to play football for the school, but I had the same problem playing football as I did playing basketball: getting back to Big Rock from after-school practice.

Coach Craig's method of dealing with fistfights and other bad behavior was interesting to me. He required the guys to put on boxing gloves, whether or not they knew how to box. He then put the two guys in the center of the gym and instructed them to fight it out while the rest of the class sat in the bleachers and watched. On more than one occasion I was instructed by Coach Craig to fight in the gym while students watched from the bleachers.

These fights ended up having a positive outcome for me, though. Because I won most of the fights and at worst held the opponents to a draw, I earned a solid measure of respect among my classmates for the remainder of my time there. There's a saying that you are only as good as your last fight. There are no pleasures in a fight, but if you have to fight, it's better if you fight to win.

The internal stress of everything, inside and outside of school, began to affect my attitude in the classroom. I made the mistake one day of speaking rudely to one of my teachers during class. The teacher asked me to read aloud to the class the next paragraph of a story we were reading and I refused. I didn't know why, but I just snapped, "No." She asked me again, and I said no again. The third time came with a warning and then I was ordered to report to the principal, Mr. Van Riggins. As outdated as it was even then, Stewart County High still believed in corporal punishment. The principal informed me that the disciplinary action for my rude behavior would consist of a paddle spanking, and he told me to bend over his desk and take my punishment. The paddle was a large one, about three feet long and six inches wide.

I refused to submit and told Mr. Van Riggins that if he struck me with the paddle I would do the same to him. I was immediately suspended and told that if I did not submit to a spanking I would be expelled from school. I was ordered off the school premises and given three days to think about it.

Mamma Pearl was upset over my suspension. The next day, she called my aunts and uncles together for a family meeting, after which Uncle Cordell placed several phone calls to the principal. Uncle Cordell, one of the best men on the planet, told me that taking the punishment would be the right thing to do. By this time I had reconsidered my position and wanted a way out of my predicament—I definitely didn't want to be expelled. Stewart County High School was the only high school in the county. There would have been nowhere else for me to go. The thought of leaving high school before graduating was intolerable to me. So when Uncle Cordell told me there was no way around the situation, I was relieved. I waited until the third day and then submitted to the spanking, which I barely felt. I returned to class more than a little embarrassed. Uncle Cordell visited me the next day to make sure I was feeling good about the decision.

By December, continuing to stay in Stewart County was no longer tenable for me. It no longer felt like the right thing. I was in my last year of high school. I had only six months to graduation and seven months to draft eligibility, and my future was still a complete unknown. I loved Stewart County, but I knew it was time to leave if I were going to take charge of my life. As much as I dreaded going back to South Seventh Street, everything inside was telling me my way was to be found in Nashville.

Like the year before, my younger brother Steve and I wrote letters back and forth between Big Rock and Nashville. In one letter I proposed that he trade places with me at Mamma Pearl's. Steve would soon be turning fifteen and I believed he would be safer in Stewart County. In a reply letter Steve agreed to my suggestion. I knew he'd experience the same kind of homesickness that I had, but I also knew that his exposure to our grandmother's strength of character and values and basic goodness would serve him well, as they had me.

When I broke the news to Mamma Pearl, she let me know she was disappointed, and tried to talk me out of it. But once it became clear to her that I'd made up my mind, she gave me her blessing. I was aiming for a life-altering change and that was not going to happen without a strong intention and the necessary footwork to go along with it.

I left at Christmas break, without telling anyone at school. I felt I had to get on with my life, and I couldn't risk being talked out of it.

CHAPTER TWENTY-SEVEN

High School Dropout

The first week of January 1967, I enrolled in East Nashville High School on Gallatin Road. Although it was the nearest high school to the projects, the school district also included neighborhoods with some of the most stately homes in East Nashville. With four stories, a clock tower, and an imposing stone facade, this classic redbrick building was the largest school I had ever attended. Immediately next door stood the junior high, which matched the high school in size and architecture. Standing side by side, the two massive buildings suggested a university campus. On my first day, walking through the arched double-doors into a swarm of students, I had a momentary attack of feeling insecure and vulnerable, unlike anything I'd felt at either Stewart County High or Cohn High near Trinity Lane.

I knew that East Nashville High had already become integrated two years before—a long eleven years after the U.S. Supreme Court's decision in *Brown v. Board of Education of Topeka* had ruled all segregated schools "inherently unequal." At East Nashville High, the first black students were scheduled to graduate with my class. But in 1967 the battle for civil rights continued on, including in Nashville. I could feel the tension as I made my way down the vast and crowded hallways of the school on the first day. With only a semester until graduation, I wondered if I had made a mistake.

I noticed right away that students were gathered into various groups awaiting the morning bell. Unlike at Stewart County, however, these students didn't separate themselves by popularity. They were separated by race. As I headed toward the registrar's office, a group of eight or ten black guys blocked my path.

"Excuse me," I said, indicating that I wanted to pass.

No one stepped aside or acknowledged my presence. Frustrated, I worked my way around them, but when I glanced back, the group was collectively staring in my direction. Their faces told me this would not be our last encounter.

By transferring in the middle of the school year, I received the usual treatment as the new kid with no friends. My few friends from South Seventh Street were either in jail or, like Bobby Sims and Danny Johnson, had dropped out of high school. Settling in wasn't helped by the fact that I had entered a large urban high school where the students had little to no discipline. From what I could see, officials at East Nashville High School seemed hesitant, almost afraid, to get involved in confrontations between students. I was used to people in leadership taking control of things, like Coach Craig making teenage boys put on boxing gloves to settle their differences, or even Mr. Van Riggins using the broad end of a paddle. Here, while the administration seemed to be doing an effective job at integrating the school, they were falling short at preventing groups from ganging up on other groups—both white and black—or using intimidation to bully their victims. Black students united against white students. Bands of white students, mostly middle-class kids, preyed on black as well as white students. An added factor that ratcheted up the tension was the Vietnam War. Regardless of color, all the senior boys were well aware of the possibility of being drafted.

Even though I'd become accustomed to gang-style violence on South Seventh Street, I hadn't expected to find that same kind of violence at school. But it was an angry time for teenagers of all colors, and by the end of my first week, I'd been involved in fights with both black students and white students. The fact that I refused to be bullied only marked me as a target for both groups.

By the third week, I was getting into two or three fistfights a day. The intimidation was nonstop. I never knew when, or with whom, the next fight would occur. I was afraid, and getting killed didn't seem outside the realm of possibility. One day between classes, a student coming down the stairs pushed me backward as I was heading up. I kept my balance, but barely. This was no accident, I realized. The guy was trying to push me down the stairwell. With a full body blow, he had attempted to force an ugly fall. Panicked, I bent forward and head-butted him in the groin. Moaning, he doubled over. Then I grabbed his belt from the rear, pulled him headfirst down the stairway, pinned him down, and made him apologize. That incident set into motion a chain of events that ultimately would devastate me.

I was facing a different kind of battleground within these school walls. From first grade on, I had learned that the only way to stop school bullies was to fight them, and this strategy had served me well over the years. But it was precisely the wrong behavior for standing up to bullies at East Nashville High School.

As it turned out, the stairwell bully belonged to a street gang, whose members hung out in groups of five or six. Like typical bullies, they aggressively bumped me in the hallways and snarled menacing threats. After the incident on the stairwell they seemed eager to extract revenge. For the next few days, the bully and his friends stalked me. I could tell they were deliberately trying to isolate me to retaliate. As long as I kept myself visible to school officials and avoided unexpected encounters, I thought I had a chance. I arrived to school early to avoid the gang, and when entering or leaving the building, I stayed aware of my surroundings, decreasing my vulnerability to an ambush.

Reluctantly, I spoke with a student counselor about the situation. He was a middle-aged, balding white male who seemed outwardly sympathetic to my problem, but offered no solution. Straight up, he informed me that I was better off trying to find a way to work the problem out on my own. As a new student, I needed time to adjust. He told me that if I gave him the names of the guys harassing me he would talk to them. But then he added, "I can't promise you that they won't retaliate."

The rest of the week passed without incident and, although I was keenly aware that I was the gang's target, I was hopeful the hostility would fade. Then one morning I walked through the front entrance of the school and saw the stairwell bully standing outside the administration office. The encounter didn't seem planned because he looked as surprised as I was. Our eyes met, and I knew the fight was on.

His attack was like a football tackle. The impact of the charge knocked me to the ground, where he placed a chokehold on me that made my neck feel like it was going to snap. I struggled to free myself from his powerful grip, but I had never been fond of wrestling and wasn't very good at it either. I was frightened that his friends would arrive at any moment and then I would really be in trouble.

We rolled back and forth on the floor. In a desperate effort to free myself from the chokehold, I punched with my elbows and kicked with my feet. Finally, I broke free and jumped to my feet. Frantically, I punched him with a flurry of left and right jabs until the fight was broken up by several students and teachers who had come running.

Afterward, I stood in front of my homeroom nervously waiting for the morning bell to ring. The stairwell bully was standing ten feet away with a clump of his buddies. The kid was in my homeroom and we shared a few classes.

"You're dead, punk," he shouted.

Later, while walking to a class, two guys approached me and said, "We'll be seeing you when school's out."

The threats continued throughout the morning. "Your time will come at three o'clock," whispered the stairwell bully later in math class.

An uninvolved student warned me that he'd heard a rumor that I was going to be stabbed as I left the school building that afternoon. At lunch, people I didn't even know told me to "get the hell out" of school right away.

As the day wore on, I tried not to think about the mess I had gotten myself into, but the pressure was too great to ignore. I watched the clock tick closer to the three o'clock bell. My mind spun. Maybe the threat against my life was a bluff. Maybe it was all bravado and posturing. Maybe it was just another fight I was facing. Should I ignore the threat, or listen to my gut and run? One thing I knew for sure: these guys were not going away. I would have to deal with them today, tomorrow, and for the rest of the school year. They had pushed the rhetoric past the point of their backing off. Street experience had taught me that boasting must be followed by action, otherwise the gang loses credibility. Moreover, the timing of the promised attack made a lot of sense to me. When school let out at three o'clock, the hallways and exit doors would be crammed with students anxious to leave the building, creating a perfect opportunity for members of the gang to attack as I exited. Such an attack could easily be coordinated by a group of determined boys covering all the exits. If they didn't get me today, then it could happen tomorrow, or at any time of their choosing.

I had learned to trust my instinct over the years, and at this moment my instinct was telling me that I was in danger of being permanently injured or being killed. Since I'd chosen to fight rather than seek a different and more successful resolution to the conflict, I had no one to blame but myself. I left the school property early that afternoon, at two-thirty, and never again returned. I had dropped out of high school.

CHAPTER TWENTY-EIGHT

Awash in Self-Doubt

I had plotted my exit carefully. A half-hour before the bell, I coolly walked out of my last class of the day and left the building by a maintenance side door. From the school grounds, I turned right and then headed toward the river, zigzagging my way to make sure I wasn't pursued. Instead of crossing over the Shelby Street Bridge, I scrambled down the bank to some rocks beneath the bridge where I sat for a long while, watching the slow-moving Cumberland and looking across to the gray, downtown skyline.

As soon as I'd walked out the door, I knew the action was final. I couldn't go back. There was no doubt in my mind of the danger the gang posed. I wasn't afraid of fighting or being beaten up. I was afraid of losing an eye, being paralyzed, or rendered disabled in some way. I was also afraid of losing my life. I wasn't afraid of death itself, because I knew I stood ready to defend my family to the death, if necessary. But no part of me was ready to die in the schoolyard.

As I sat on the riverbank, chilled to the bone, my hands buried in my pockets, I began to grieve having lost my high school diploma. It felt like the end of the road for me. I felt like just another hapless dropout. And no matter how much I tried to justify my leaving school, to blame it on the stairwell bully and his cohorts, I knew that I had played a part. The moment I grabbed the guy on the stairs in retaliation, I had opened the door to the ensuing consequences. I knew better, but by fighting back, especially on unknown turf, I had chosen to take the wrong action, the unwise course, the self-destructive course.

On a dark road five years before, a blaze of light had presented itself to me—a presence that I couldn't explain in ordinary words, then or now, a higher power or God—that awakened me to the existence of pure love and that infused me with the feeling of intense peace and innocence. My contact with this presence or spirit was a profound gift of reassurance. At twelve years old, I couldn't have framed this experience as a turning point, but that's exactly what it was and has continued to be. And with this came a moral center, a new awareness of right and wrong—not wrong in the sense of any inherent guilt but rather in the sense of poor choices, actions misaligned with my better judgment, or better self. With respect to this, an inner struggle ensued almost at once having to do with fighting. From that time on, every fight I had, no matter what the circumstances, filled me with remorse. In the past five years, I had chosen to fight over and over again and, each time, even on South Seventh Street with all its horrors, I suffered the weight of remorse.

Fighting and remorse were synonymous for me, an inseparable pair. I never started a fight, but that fact didn't seem to ease the regret that accompanied any fight I took part in. Plain and simple, fighting for me was a bad choice, but often—usually—my first choice. I went out of my way to avoid confrontation, but when directly threatened, I enjoyed feeling the power of my fist. I enjoyed the pride of winning. I liked feeling like a warrior. Aside from the love and guidance of my mother and grandmother, fighting had been my principal training for life up to that time.

After it grew dark, I walked for a while before going home. I kept the truth from my family, at least for that night.

The following morning, I left at the usual time under the pretense of going to school. Instead, I walked all the way to downtown Nashville, where I meandered aimlessly for the day. I had hours to kill, so I walked the waterfront, among the well-dressed men and women in the business district, and Music Row, where RCA's Studio B recorded Elvis's hit single "Heartbreak Hotel." I felt lost. There was nowhere to run to or hide from the emotions that were sticking to me. Passing Woolworth's, I saw a blind black man playing guitar and singing the blues for pocket change. From working the parking lots, I'd seen him quite a bit downtown. For a guitar strap, he always used a worn-out waist belt. I stopped and listened, feeling ashamed of my own depression. I was worried to the point of exhaustion. I was awash in self-doubt. I had fallen into a black hole.

CHAPTER TWENTY-NINE

Standing Up to Father

I felt lost after dropping out of high school, and I stayed lost for a good part of that year. I found work right away but felt as though I were in a void. It was like being in exile. I didn't belong anywhere. At East Nashville High School, I had felt far removed from the world of the white, mostly middle-class kids. I didn't even feel like I belonged to my own generation, who were angry not just about the Vietnam War and racial inequality but also about the whole value system of mainstream society, of their parents' generation. As part of the underclass, my priority was basic survival, and the constant need to work created a disconnection between my life and what was happening with my more moneyed peers. My best hope was to make it into the very mainstream of society that my generation was rejecting. I was trying to fit in; they were trying to opt out. I was trying to get away from violence; they were exploring it for the first time. Although I couldn't have articulated it then,

I was twice removed from "the city on the hill"—I wasn't part of the "real" society, the place with the "real" jobs, nor was I part of the new generation critiquing it. From where I stood, the protest generation was itself mainstream. It stood on a bedrock of economic stability that I could only dream about.

In the meantime, I could identify with the discrimination felt by blacks, and also with the poor blacks and whites who were being sent to Vietnam by the hundreds of thousands.

I also identified strongly with the music. Music reduced my extreme feelings of isolation. It helped me to understand the countercultural attitudes surrounding me, especially the music of Bob Dylan, who cut his album *Blonde on Blonde* in Nashville. Dylan's lyrics came straight at me, and taught me everything I needed to know about my generation's anger and discontent and sensitivity. I was also passionate about Jimi Hendrix and Janis Joplin. Jimi Hendrix, with his hit single "Hey, Joe," introduced a whole new funky guitar sound that grabbed me, along with the lead lyric "Hey, Joe, where you goin' with that gun in your hand." I envisioned myself carrying a rifle in Vietnam. Dropping out of high school made it a near certainty that I'd be drafted. Sometimes I would change the lyrics to "Hey, Doug, where you goin' with that gun in your hand." I'd sing it with humor to cover up my fear of being a potential victim in an unpopular war.

Janis Joplin was lead singer in the band Big Brother and the Holding Company. I first noticed her raspy, bluesy, soulful singing with "Down on Me"—"Down on me, down on me, looks like everybody in the whole round world, they're down on me." Janis's lifestyle was wild and out of control and I could relate to that, as well as to what seemed to be an aching deficit of self-esteem.

I also loved the music coming from England, in particular, the Beatles—*Rubber Soul*—and the Rolling Stones—*Out of Our Heads*. For some reason, there was social pressure to choose between the two, but I liked them equally. I didn't own a stereo but I had a radio, and in idle moments, when I wasn't working, I hung out at the famous

Hippodrome Roller Rink across the river on West End Avenue. The Hippodrome always had a playlist I could count on.

I worked relentlessly, but for the first time fell into a pattern of getting jobs, working for a while, and then quitting. Jumping from job to job wasn't normal for me, but nothing was normal for me then. I might quit because I didn't like the boss or found fault with the company's attitude. Fortunately, there were plenty of jobs, so I was never without one. Mostly, I think I quit because I was angry. I was angry because I was separated from the mainstream of society by a wide difference in social status. I was trying to catch up to a society impossible to catch up to.

In early summer Bracy received a hardship discharge from the air force, an honorable discharge granted to soldiers who had to return home to help support their families. Mom had signed the affidavits certifying the need for her son's support. It had been a year, and I was excited to see him.

We started spending a lot of time together, even though Bracy rarely stayed a night at the apartment. We teamed up finding jobs. The two of us worked together in a number of different factories—making shoe boxes, cabinets, and fiberglass. We hated working with fiberglass—it got inside our hair, our clothes, our shoes, and even our skin. We left that job after a few weeks.

We worked as a team and we quit as a team. For me, on good days, I considered every job temporary because my attitude was that I'd be leaving it behind when I went to college. When my boss at the shoe-box factory wanted to give me a promotion, I quit the same day. Accepting the promotion would have been an acknowledgment that I didn't have a better option awaiting me.

I liked having Bracy as a work partner. We hung out together outside of work too. I felt peaceful and happy around him, but I worried about him, as I did all of my siblings.

Soon after our younger brother Steve had come home from Mamma Pearl's for the summer, he got hurt pretty badly. He was stopped at a red light in the neighborhood with his window rolled down, when he was smashed in the face with a broken beer bottle by a passerby. The passerby turned out to be someone he'd beaten in a fight a few weeks earlier. A huge gash left a four-inch zigzag facial scar that looked like a lightning bolt.

Meanwhile, life at home was chaotic and in a constant state of crisis. Mom was still working full-time at a job that paid the minimum wage. To save on transportation cost she had taken a factory job within walking distance of our home at the Davis Cabinet Company. Bracy and I turned over part of our paychecks, as did Steve. Our father remained a deadbeat. Since I had come home from Stewart County the previous December, he and I had been skirting around a serious clash, although, as usual, I was doing everything possible to keep it from happening.

One day I came home from work to find my father and my uncle Wesley in the living room. They were both drunk and giving Mom a hard time. Uncle Wes was Mom's younger brother and had a reputation as a mean drunk who often started fights and was quick to use a knife. As a child, I had always been afraid of him.

I took a seat and listened as my father barked orders at Mom to fix sandwiches and bring beers, using foul language and abusive gestures. Making it worse, Uncle Wes joined in. The two of them together were more than I could stand and I had the impression that they'd cranked it up a notch for my benefit just as I entered the house, an intentional in-your-face aggravation. My father allowing Uncle Wes to speak so crudely to Mom was like adding gasoline to fire for me. Mom seemed nervous, no doubt because she could tell that I was angry. She would always put her child first, before herself.

Seething inside, I continued to watch. I felt someone was going to have to put a stop to the mistreatment, so I silently plotted my strategy. The two men were seated together on the couch, at a right angle to my chair. I would have to take out Uncle Wes first, as the more unpredictable and rabid of the two. I pretended not to object to his horrid behavior, even managing a smile when he looked my way. Patience was of the essence. Making a move too early would risk both of them jumping on me at once.

Eventually, Uncle Wes struggled off the couch to go to the bathroom. I stood up and slipped behind him in a single beat, simultaneously flicking the knife out of my right pocket. I placed the open blade firmly against his throat. "Make a move and you will die," I said.

"What the hell?" he drawled, in a high-pitched voice. I'd taken him by surprise. I glanced at my father, who had the same caught look on his face that I'd seen the day the bootlegger taught him a lesson. He sat unmoving on the couch.

Slowly, still pressing the knife against his neck, I sidled Uncle Wes to the front door, while I held him tightly with my left arm. At the door, I said, "Time for you to go" and pushed him out with a solid kick. He toppled facedown. I replaced the knife into my pocket.

My uncle stirred and tried to rise. I moved closer and stood over him. "You come back here again and one of us will die," I said. When he slacked off, I stepped back cautiously, allowing him to get up. He shambled away without looking back, heading down South Seventh in the direction of his place a few blocks away. As I watched him go, I remembered Mamma Pearl once saying to me, "If you make the right enemies, you are living a good life." Uncle Wes was the right enemy.

My anger unabated, I walked back into the apartment where my father continued to sit in a fog of alcohol. I blamed my father for every single thing gone wrong with our family. I desperately wanted to throw him out.

"This stuff you are doing, it's going to stop now," I said to him, looking him straight in the eyes.

"Don't think you're too tough to get your ass whipped," he sneered.

"Fine, let's do it right now," I said. I was ready for this moment. I'd been ready for this moment for a decade and now there was no stopping me. I had little doubt that I could handle the confrontation.

"Please don't fight," pleaded Mom. That stopped me. I pulled back and sat down. I took a breath. My eyes remained locked with my father's, each of us assessing the other's possible first move.

"You have two choices," I said to him. "You respect Mom or you can fight me." In deference to Mom, I spoke with deliberate calm and kept the rhetoric toned down.

All of a sudden, we were interrupted by a loud voice at the door, "Doug, you better come out here, there is a guy coming after you with a knife."

I ran outside and saw Uncle Wes running fast in my direction with a butcher knife in his hand. He was about a hundred feet away. Without a thought, I started running toward him at full speed, at which point he stopped, pivoted, and proceeded to run even faster in the opposite direction. I chased him for a while, but just to let him know that I wasn't afraid of him.

By the time I returned home, my father had gone upstairs to the bathroom. Mom implored me not to do anything I would later regret.

I went outside and sat on the front steps. I remember that I was wearing a T-shirt and it was a hot summer night and still light out. I sat with my back to the open door. I could hear my father's footsteps as he walked down the stairs and toward me out the front door. He stopped immediately behind my back. I wondered if he held a knife, but realized it didn't matter. *Whatever happens is meant to happen,* I thought.

My father was so close that I could hear his breathing and feel the cuffs of his pants brushing lightly against the edge of my back. I was not afraid. It was a strange moment for me. I did what I thought was right at the time. I remained seated without turning around.

"Like I said, you have two choices," I told him, still standing behind me. I wasn't going to back away and I wanted him to know that his behavior had to change if we were going to continue living in the same house together.

"And what are you going to do?" he mocked. It was a curious and bold comment, perhaps even a threat. Again, I wondered if he had a knife. Still, I felt calm, safe.

"You know the answer to that," I said. This time I was mocking him.

A long moment passed with neither one of us saying another word. And then I heard my father walk back into the house.

That was it. The conflict was over. My father left a few days later and went back to Stewart County.

I never saw Uncle Wes again. He died some years later of liver disease, brought on by alcohol abuse.

In facing down my father, I was standing my ground on the right of our family to live a normal and peaceful life. In the days following our father's departure we slowly settled into a routine that restored some measure of peace and happiness in our home. But the family struggled. Mom supported her children by continuing to work the minimum wage job at Davis Cabinet Company. Dad, true to his character, refused to pay child support. Despite the financial uncertainty, my spirits were strangely uplifted. Knowing that Mom was safe was like a heavy weight lifted from my shoulders. I felt a greater sense of purpose, a focused responsibility to provide financial support for my mother. To do that I knew I had to get my life back on track. I turned my attention back to the business of continuing my education.

PART THREE

Moving On

CHAPTER THIRTY

The Job Corps

On July 15, I turned eighteen. I was driving a delivery truck for a small butcher shop, another dead-end job, and spinning my wheels trying to get my life back on track. My mind was as chaotic as my circumstances. In the meantime, my former senior class at East Nashville had graduated without me and I had become fresh meat for the draft.

I clung to the only plan I had, which was to get my GED as soon as possible. I was about to start the preparatory course for the exam when, in "a simple twist of fate," to quote Bob Dylan, my life took a wild turn.

This happened to be one of those times that our family had a working black-and-white television. I was watching the news after work. As usual it was dominated by horrific images from Southeast Asia, footage of dead and injured American soldiers being evacuated by helicopter out of the jungles of Vietnam. During a commercial break, my attention was caught by a thirty-second spot advertising something called the Job Corps. I'd never heard of the Job Corps, but the ad described it as an alternative for youths who had dropped out of high school. I didn't have to write it down; it seemed like it was an opportunity designed especially for me.

The next morning, I found the address for the Job Corps in the Nashville phone book, and then took a bus downtown to the office in the federal building on Broadway. A quite meticulous man in his forties went thoroughly through my application with me, checking and double-checking each answer. I had answered "no" to having any prior criminal record and when he asked me again if the answer was correct, my conscience wouldn't let me lie, so I told him about being involved in the theft of five gallons of gasoline. I was worried this would derail me, but the man said it wouldn't "pose a problem." I made it clear to him that I was ready to join the Job Corps immediately. Because I was eighteen, no parental permission was required. I was able to make all my decisions on the spot and sign all the paperwork on that very day.

The program sounded too good to be true. Initially conceived by Sargent Shriver and a central part of Lyndon Baines Johnson's War on Poverty, it had only been around for four years and was free to young people sixteen to twenty-four who were in need of further education and had limited financial resources. I qualified. It was a live-in program that provided education, job training, career counseling, and, what especially attracted me, the opportunity to earn a GED at no cost.

This was a no-nonsense operation. My paperwork was processed in a few short weeks. I was accepted, and in early August I boarded a Greyhound bus heading for the McCoy Job Corps Center at a retired army base on the outskirts of the small town of Sparta, Wisconsin, seven hundred miles away from Nashville. On the long bus ride north I felt at ease and excited. I felt committed to make this work. I *needed* to make it work. The thought of ending up in a lifetime of blind-alley jobs like other high school dropouts was unbearable, as was ending up a soul-sick drunk like my father. I'd learned that the Job Corps had been modeled on the Depression-era Civilian Conservation Corps, or

CCC. As a young man in the 1930s, my father had been one of its dropouts. Now here I was thirty years later, his son, trying for the same chance. May I make it, I prayed.

Camp McCoy, formerly known as Camp Robinson, had served as a major training facility during both World War II and the Korean War. It was a huge military base, but it was mostly vacant now except as a training center for the National Guard and the Job Corps. Just a year before I arrived, the military had leased barracks and other buildings to the Job Corps, as well as acres of woods and lush evergreens that reminded me of Stewart County.

From the Greyhound bus station in Sparta, a military bus transported a group of us out to the base. All the new Job Corps arrivals were housed together in two-story, white-clapboard army barracks, each furnished with metal bunk beds, army blankets, and pillows. Each of the barracks housed about fifty corpsmen. Camp McCoy itself was sectioned into seven "neighborhoods" of three or four barracks each. Two hundred corpsmen might make up a neighborhood. For the first week, all new arrivals lived together while attending orientation classes, after which each of us would be randomly assigned to a neighborhood.

The first night, after dinner in the mess hall with a sea of other corpsmen, I did my best to get settled along with the other new arrivals in my barracks. This first night turned out to be a revelation of huge proportion for me. Almost all fifty of us stayed up well past midnight talking about why we had decided to join the Job Corps. The conversation started out among just a few of us on the second floor, and one by one, the whole barracks gathered together, some guys on their bunks, some standing, some sitting on the floor. The whole center aisle was soon packed with corpsmen from all over the United States, mostly from big cities like Chicago, Atlanta, and Philly. Outside it was pitch dark, but we'd left the ceiling lights on and the door open for August night breezes.

I listened closely and realized that I was relating to everything my barracks-mates were saying. I told my own story, too. There was no separation between them and me. We were brothers. The majority of us came from dysfunctional and alcoholic families who lived in government-subsidized housing projects. We'd known a lifetime of poverty and absent fathers. We had failed to complete high school. We'd hit bottom. We felt this might be our last chance. Everyone wanted the same thing: we wanted our twisted lives to go straight.

Outside of my family, this was the first time in my life that I felt like I belonged among a group of individuals. The *first* time. Everything clicked into place. It was an emotional moment for me. I was the only white guy in the barracks, but I was them and they were me. We were the same.

The next morning, Monday, orientation classes began—the instruction focused on the rules and objectives of the Job Corps. I was riveted. I wanted to know just how everything was going to work. At noon our instructor, a twenty-five-year-old college graduate from the Midwest, led our class to the gigantic mess hall where meals were served. Altogether, there were probably twelve hundred of us. We had been waiting in line for about twenty-five minutes, inching forward just close enough to see the food on the buffet, when a corpsman, without explanation, cut in front of me.

I tapped him on the shoulder. "Excuse me, the line starts back there," I pointed. The corpsman was about six feet two, well muscled, and closer to age twenty-four than sixteen. And by his worn uniform, I could tell he wasn't new.

He turned around and I felt the full weight of his stony gaze and hands as he shoved me in the chest and said, "What are you going to do about it?"

Without thinking, I shoved him back. He stumbled backward, knocking over a chair, which attracted the attention of a security guard who stepped in just as the guy came charging back at me. The guard ordered the corpsman to the back of the line.

"You better hope you don't get assigned to Neighborhood 7 or you will be one dead white boy," the corpsman said, with a final, steely-eyed look.

Why hadn't I just let the guy cut in line? I thought, angry at myself. Here it was my first full day in the Job Corps and it was like being back on the street in East Nashville. The episode ruined my appetite. I could feel the eyes of the big corpsman drilling into the back of my head. My stomach ached, and not from a lack of food. I promised myself that no matter what happened, I would not fight. I would do everything in my power to keep things right before they went wrong.

"May I have the strength to do what's right," I prayed that night.

The remainder of orientation week went smoothly and without incident. On Friday, all of us gathered to receive our neighborhood assignments. Of course, my preference was that my assignment not be Neighborhood 7, but I was prepared to go forward regardless. During the week, I had learned that fighting was strictly prohibited in the Job Corps, with stiff penalties for those caught violating the rule. Fighting was cause for immediate expulsion, and was the number one reason that corpsmen left the camp. This gave me some comfort— maybe the angry corpsman's threat hadn't been real. From what I'd observed so far, most of the guys were trying for a fresh start. But I was prepared to do whatever was necessary to complete the program. My determination was so strong that I felt nothing was going to stop me from finishing the job that I had come here to do.

The instructor came into our barracks and began to call out the neighborhood assignments in alphabetical order by last name. His cadence was that of a man who had been through this routine many times before. One by one he rattled off the names and assignments with the rhythm of a drill sergeant. As he neared the end of the alphabet, I heard "Wallace, Douglas, Neighborhood 7."

I wasn't surprised. All summer, I had asked God for a second chance in life, and that was exactly what I was getting. I hadn't asked God to make it any easier on me the second time around. So it was fitting that I should be faced with similar choices, and the opportunity to choose differently. This time I would not run, nor would I fight. I was willing to go to Neighborhood 7 as assigned.

As we packed our uniforms and other gear, an older man walked into the barracks dressed like an army captain, maybe in his mid-sixties. He wore the double silver bars on his khaki uniform, but the patch on his sleeve bore the letters CP. We all listened as he explained that he was captain of the Job Corps security team, known as the Courtesy Patrol. Its function was to patrol the neighborhoods to make sure the rules were abided by. He was there to recruit volunteers for the team. The job paid no money, nor did it provide extra credit toward graduation. Furthermore, it required working extra hours at night and on weekends. But the CP officers lived in their own neighborhood. Maybe I wasn't meant to be in Neighborhood 7 after all. Maybe my second chance was accepting the captain's offer. My hand shot up, startling the captain, I think. I was one of the four new corpsmen who joined the Courtesy Patrol that day.

My first three weeks were intense. My time was divided between training for the Courtesy Patrol and attending regular classes. The CP course included running, weight-training, and martial arts techniques, all of which I relished. It taught the use of a billy bat as well, but the primary training was in skillful means for dealing with any corpsman sliding into violence, usually in a fight. We operated as a team, patrolling in groups of four. When a fight broke out, we tried to calm down those fighting and did everything we could to help the corpsmen avoid detention, or even expulsion. We were more like mentors than police. "Come on, you don't want to get kicked out of the Job Corps—let it go," would be a typical exchange between a CP officer and a corpsman acting out.

The stated purpose of the CP officer was to protect the corpsmen and preserve the camp structure so we could each accomplish what we'd come to the Job Corps to do. For the first time in my life, I was part of a society specifically structured to facilitate and enable disadvantaged youths to learn how to live peacefully and productively.

Since most of the corpsmen in the Job Corps were desperately seeking a second chance, the need for security was less than I would have expected from street-tough boys and men. Like me, they had the swagger and hardened faces of fighters, but, here, we had stood down. We weren't staring each other down or flexing our muscles or practicing intimidation. It was an uncanny sensation to be among battle-primed individuals acknowledging their failures and showing their vulnerable sides. The only exception to this, as it turned out, was Neighborhood 7. If CP duty hadn't been made available, I most certainly would have been in trouble.

Being a CP officer meant more work, but I had never shied away from hard work. CP officers not only shared a barracks, but we were also held to a higher standard and lived with closer supervision. For me, this was an advantage. I needed the rules and regulations and thrived in the structured environment that encouraged me to progress at my own speed, without the distractions of violence or prejudice. We had three solid meals a day, I was using my mind on something beyond fighting, and I was empowered to take the initiative to reach for things that had eluded me. I started sailing.

By early October, I had studied for and taken the GED test. Also, by that time I had learned that the Job Corps assisted corpsmen in gaining admission to college, as well as applying for financial assistance. This I hadn't expected. I established the goal for myself of entering college no later than January. Certain Job Corps centers around the country had cooperative agreements with community and vocational colleges. But I was fortunate to be stationed at the only center that had an agreement with a four-year university system, the University of Wisconsin. The quiet spirit within me was saying, "Yes, you see, everything will be all right."

CHAPTER THIRTY-ONE

Breaking Through the Barrier

The Job Corps relied upon its instructors to determine the pace at which corpsmen could advance though the program. Most corpsmen took between one to two years to graduate. Some required longer. My goal to be admitted to college for the January semester was definitely an accelerated pace. The Corps counselors believed I was making a mistake to set such an aggressive goal for myself. But I was adamant and succeeded in winning the support of a key counselor, Jeff Dillon, who agreed to help me on the condition that various instructors sign off on my completion of their courses. That was a strict requirement, as was a high school diploma. I hadn't yet received my GED scores.

I got along well with all my instructors—all except for one. I had a big problem with the woman who taught data processing. From the first day in class, it had been obvious that I wasn't Mrs. Tripp's favorite student. I didn't know how bad it was until she called me aside one day and said, "You will never graduate from this class."

This mean-spirited, degrading comment took me by surprise and was completely out of character for Job Corps staff. I didn't say anything, but it cut deeply. Without her support, my plan to graduate early would come to a screeching halt. I kept my mouth shut for the rest of the class that day and fought back humiliating tears.

In the barracks that night I told the CP captain what had happened and asked for his help. He had no authority over my instructors, but he offered to talk to them in order to determine my standing in their classrooms. A few days later he called me into his office. He said he wanted our conversation to be held in confidence. He had spoken to each of my teachers. Only Mrs. Tripp had a problem with my early graduation. He suggested that my too-confident attitude may have offended her and advised me to show her more deference, to exhibit a little humility in her classroom. "Make things right by offering a general and sincere apology for your overall behavior in her class," he said, "Something like, 'I'm sorry and sincerely regret if my behavior in class has in any way offended you.'"

The next day I scheduled an appointment with Mrs. Tripp, during which I repeatedly apologized. I ended up pouring my heart out to her in our twenty-minute meeting, acknowledging frankly that she bore a huge measure of control over my destiny. She seemed appreciative of the apology but remained cool.

For the next two months, I did my best to act friendly, even groveling, toward this instructor. I had my eye on the prize. Finally, she called me aside one day to say that my graduation from her class was a certainty. Lesson learned: if making the right enemies means you're doing something right, making the wrong enemies means you're doing something wrong.

In November my GED scores came in. I passed—I had earned my high school diploma. I applied for admission to several Wisconsin colleges. My counselor, Jeff, and other Job Corps staff were helpful beyond measure in this process. They wrote letters of recommendation on my behalf, made phone calls to directors of admissions, and began the laborious task of helping me to apply for financial aid. Things began to happen very quickly. I was still attending classes and, in addition, submitting to interviews and evaluations by Job Corps personnel as they considered my application for accelerated graduation. There were many variables in play and virtually no precedence at the Job Corps for what I was trying to do.

At Camp McCoy, the Job Corps population was 95 percent black. Among the new arrivals, I had been the only white in my barracks. Among the CP officers, I was also the only white, but we refused to be divided along racial lines.

Night after night, the television networks played and replayed scenes of white police officers beating up on black protestors in cities like Detroit and Newark. Our barracks had a TV on the first floor. I could see the disgust and anger on the faces of my fellow corpsmen as they watched. These guys were my closest friends; some were like brothers to me. Listening to their own stories, I understood why any young black man would doubt the motivation of white police officers. Some of the corpsmen spoke of outrageous discrimination happening in their hometowns, but police abuse and misconduct seemed to upset them the most.

At Camp McCoy, we were living in a rarefied environment in a way, far away from the streets, but the streets were still a part of us. What was happening outside couldn't help but boil over onto the base. On a few occasions, as security, we were put on "alert status." A dusk-to-dawn curfew might be imposed for a night. But mostly the Job Corps administrators considered corpsmen's shouts and protests as blowing off steam, which cooled off in a matter of hours with no one seriously hurt. Camp McCoy was the real beginning of my education on race relations in our country and the realization of how far we had to go to rectify the wrongs.

In early December, the University of Wisconsin in Eau Claire let me know that it was considering my admission for the January semester. Several weeks later, my acceptance was made official, along with a complete financial aid package. I graduated from the Job Corps six days before Christmas.

CHAPTER THIRTY-TWO

Exploding Coke Bottle

I n January 1968 I started classes at the University of Wisconsin at Eau Claire, a large campus on the Chippewa River and on the edge of the Chippewa Valley. The small city of Eau Claire, French for "clear water," is two hundred and fifty miles northwest of Milwaukee and ninety miles east of the twin cities of St. Paul and Minneapolis, which lie across the border in Minnesota. The hundreds of trees scattered across the campus, from saplings to full-grown firs, were covered in snow when I arrived. Ten thousand students were enrolled in the university.

My financial aid package combined grants, loans, and a work-study program that covered my tuition and housing. I was assigned to a boarding house eight blocks from campus. I had hoped to live in a dormitory, but halfway through the year, all the dorms were filled to capacity. The financial aid people arranged off-campus housing for me in a tidy 1930s house with a chimney and dormer windows that was one of many on a street of boarding houses. On the second floor were three student rooms, two of them already occupied by upperclassmen. Mine was a corner unit with a single bed, a two-drawer dresser, a closet, and a small desk. The main part of the house downstairs—the kitchen and living room—was off-limits. The stairs to our quarters led directly from the front foyer. Because my room was tucked into a corner, I had windows on two walls, which I would leave open an inch or so for fresh air. I preferred to keep my room cool at nights, even in winter, which I think had to do with growing up in shacklike houses that were barely shelter and perennially open to the out-of-doors.

Right off, the landlady, who wore glasses and a cranky expression, told me that she didn't like having been assigned a freshman. I was allowed to have soft drinks in my room but not food. She warned me that no alcohol was permitted inside her home, and that I could not invite friends into my room. That was fine with me because I was happy just to be there.

With UW Eau Claire I had landed in exactly the right school at the right time. The university's bold admissions policy sought to overcome disparities in wealth, privilege, and power in keeping with the university's philosophy that all students have inherent dignity and worth, regardless of race or economic background. It was this progressive policy to diversify the freshman class that had opened the doorway for my admission to Eau Claire. And it was Eau Claire that rescued me from the prison of poverty.

Nothing in my background had prepared me for the experience I was about to have. I was the first member of my family to go to college. When I walked onto the Eau Claire campus for the first time, I felt an overwhelming sense of gratification and, at the same time, trepidation. I had reached the milepost—I carried my college ID card with pride. But I was also stepping onto completely unknown turf. Academically, the ground looked smooth. Socially, the terrain looked rocky. I hadn't been groomed for the easygoing, anything-goes lifestyle of a college campus. I felt like a stranger in a strange land.

Even the cold took on a whole new meaning for me in Wisconsin. I had never known bone-shattering winters like those in Eau Claire, where the average daily winter temperature was twelve degrees Fahrenheit and a good day was twenty. Barely two weeks after the semester began, a cold snap hit during the night. If Wisconsin is having a cold snap, you know it's bad. I was asleep when a frigid shock awakened me to some serious shivering. I sprinted to close the windows and jumped back into bed, wrapping my body as tightly as I could in the blankets. Unable to go back to sleep, I got up, put on another layer of clothing, and sat up in bed until first light.

The morning was dark and overcast and the clouds looked heavy with more snow. A foot or more of snow already lay on the ground. Out the window, people were going about their business as usual, seemingly unfazed by the icy siege. Obviously, in a place where winter lasts five months, people learn to adapt. Everyone was wearing oversize boots, bulky wool hats pulled down over their ears, and colorful, heavy wool scarves wrapped around their necks and faces so that only their eyes were visible. Long wool coats covered the multiple layers of clothing underneath, making everyone look slightly overweight. You could hardly distinguish males from females. Plumes of breath issued from everybody's mouth.

My four months at Camp McCoy had toughened me to a bitter, dry cold. But because Eau Claire stood alongside a river and among hills that served as wind tunnels, the cold there was far more fierce. As it turned out, on that particular morning, the windchill temperature had plunged to *minus* sixty degrees Fahrenheit. That kind of cold can eat you alive. I was completely unprepared for winter weather of that magnitude. My only coat was the brown, military-style, hip-length jacket of medium-weight wool that I'd been given in the Job Corps. I knew it wasn't sufficient for zero and sub-zero temperatures. I began to worry about having to walk to school every day in the weather.

That morning I layered up with two pairs of pants, two shirts, a sweater, and my jacket, and then grabbed my books and left the boarding house. I was wearing a pair of high-cut military boots, also from the Job Corps. As soon as I stepped out the front door I knew I was in trouble. The cold slammed into me. I was hit with an icy wind instantly painful to my cheeks, nose, chin, and even my eyes. My fingers and feet went numb before I was halfway down the street. It was like wearing only a bathing suit and plunging into an arctic river. My body stiffened and resisted my will to walk on. I swung around and hurried back to the house, where I redressed myself with two more pairs of socks—I would have added more but then my boots wouldn't have fit—another sweater for a scarf, and more socks as gloves, just like I used to do as a boy in Stewart County.

The second time I completed the eight-block walk to school, but it was a torturous journey. I stopped at the first campus building I came to and, in order to thaw out my feet, removed my boots and socks and put them on a heater to warm them up. Then, once in a class, I had to layer down quickly because I grew suddenly hot inside the stifling classroom. All day long I dreaded the trip back home. Fortunately, as part of my financial aid package, I had a meal ticket that enabled me to eat three meals a day in the school cafeteria. This enabled me to remain on campus until just before dark, and then I had to make the miserable trek back to the boarding house.

The wretched weather persisted for several weeks. Each time I left the heated indoors I worried about frostbite around my face, hands, and feet. I planned my trips to and from school carefully, and I spent a lot of time studying in the school library.

One day I returned to the boarding house and the landlady was waiting for me in the entry foyer. "Did you place a Coke bottle on the windowsill?" she asked with tightened lips.

"Yes," I said.

"Well, it exploded!" she said, with obvious irritation. Sourly, she told me that she'd spent all morning cleaning up the mess and accused me of deliberately causing damage to her home. Clearly, she was upset, so I tried to explain that I had never experienced such cold weather, had no way of knowing the bottle would explode, and that I'd only placed the Coke on the sill to keep it cold. She refused to accept my explanation and told me that I had a day to vacate the room. She never wavered from her belief that I had plotted to torment her. The next morning, unable to change her mind, I left the boarding house, a heavy suitcase in one hand, books in the other, and made my way to school. I had to make several stops to warm my hands and catch my breath. Moreover, the suitcase was in bad shape and popped open at one point, spilling my clothes out onto the snow. I hastily repacked and used my belt to bind the suitcase. The cold, the snow, the ice, and the wind were conspiring with the landlady to compound my misery.

I must have looked pathetic when I walked into the financial aid office that morning because immediately I received the sympathy of the staff. They were unhappy with the landlady's eviction for such a trivial reason. My greatest concern had been that I might somehow be expelled for this incident. I had been at Eau Claire for less than two months. Instead, within hours, I was assigned a room on campus inside the North Tower, a new dormitory overlooking the river. I had been spared by a random act of kindness, a recurring theme that mysteriously shaped my destiny.

CHAPTER THIRTY-THREE

Learning Middle-Class Behavior

My roommate in the dorm was a Chinese foreign exchange student. He was not happy that I had moved in. He'd had the room to himself until then and seemed to resent my sudden intrusion upon his private living quarters. But I was so relieved that I remained in good standing as a student that whether or not I had a friendly roommate didn't matter to me all that much. Cho spent most of his free time hanging out with other Chinese students at the university.

As new students, I think both of us were experiencing our own kind of culture shock. It was Cho's first time in America and he was clearly struggling with the language and the customs of this country. At the same time, in many ways, I was still the kid from the housing projects looking over my shoulder. I was still the poorest kid in Stewart County. My social naiveté and lack of sophistication in this university setting was pronounced. For example, I had never before used deodorant. I thought you applied it directly *onto* the shirt, underneath the armpits. Cho must have thought I was crazy when he saw me using deodorant for the first time. Like Cho, I needed time to adjust, and our months together as roommates were awkward. We had no way of explaining ourselves to each other. It was only because we both seemed to make an effort to avoid the other that we managed to remain as roommates for the rest of the semester without a fistfight. That was progress for me.

My classes varied from business to liberal arts. My favorite subjects were American literature and music. I felt at home in the classroom. During that first semester, it was one of the few places on campus where I fit like a glove, thrived, and felt like I had a good measure of control. I remember my first writing assignment was on *The Great Gatsby* by F. Scott Fitzgerald—I got an A on that paper. We read Henry David Thoreau and Henry Wadsworth Longfellow, among other American writers. I was a fast, prolific reader. Homework assignments were not a problem. I spent a lot of time in the library. I had never before been in the presence of so many books, floor to ceiling, and felt like I'd wasted so much time. In the library building were small listening rooms, where I heard the powerful music of Beethoven, Bach, and Mozart for the first time.

More than halfway through the term, on April 4, Martin Luther King was assassinated. His loss affected me profoundly, as I knew it did my friends back in the Job Corps. I was afraid that Dr. King's cause would be lost along with him. He stood for equal justice and equal rights for people of all races, and that included me. I felt like he was speaking to me as much as to people of his own color. I wanted to reach that mountaintop alongside him. He articulated the dreams of the deprived and offered a new vision for dealing with poverty.

I had been a white recipient of the current administration's approach to housing the poor: crowded, dismal government housing projects that are nothing but breeding grounds for future felons and hopelessness. I had seen what the housing projects had done, and were still doing, to my family. Dr. King had given me hope. We were just finishing up spring semester when Robert Kennedy was assassinated, two months after Dr. King, on June 5.

It was 1968 and, like every other college campus in the nation, Eau Claire had its share of protests, although there the Vietnam War seemed to overshadow the issues of civil rights. And, as I had felt disconnected from my peers at East Nashville High School, at college the disconnect was magnified, perhaps because we were older and the arena was bigger. I didn't share the antiestablishment sentiment of many of my college classmates. I was pursuing the American dream when, for them, that dream was obsolete. They were into drugs; I was into being clean. Violence had become an acceptable form of protest; I had had enough violence to last me a lifetime. Protest was their solution; it wasn't the solution to any of my problems. My generation wanted freedom from rules; I was seeking the how-to-make-a-life instruction booklet that seemed to have been distributed to everybody but the underclass. They were starting from the middle on up; I was starting from the bottom. Their struggle was about remaking society; my struggle was about remaking myself, and Eau Claire, in spite of differences of direction, was a very good place for that.

I had to learn a completely new way of life. I had to reject what I had learned from the schoolyard and the street about survival. I had to change my bad boy behavior and bad boy image. I had to find skillful, more peaceful means of communicating. I knew it wouldn't happen overnight, so I kept imagining Mamma Pearl counseling patience.

When the semester ended I enrolled in summer school full-time in order to catch up with the freshmen class. The dormitory was closed for the summer, so I found a room for rent in one of the local fraternities. The fraternity house had a full kitchen, which helped lower my food costs considerably. From Mom, I had learned how to stretch a dollar by buying in bulk. So I bought seventy-five pounds of potatoes, twenty pounds of flour, a large bag of frozen chicken parts, and ten pounds of lard—all for less than fifty dollars—enough food to feed me for the entire summer. I prepared every meal, which usually consisted of some combination of bread, gravy, potatoes, and chicken. I had a lot of biscuits and gravy.

For my summer job I worked in the university's maintenance department mowing lawns, pruning trees, and cleaning the campus grounds. In the winter I worked in the cafeteria. The thing about the work-study program was that all of your earnings went directly toward tuition. No cash changed hands. So, to pick up a few dollars, on weekends throughout the school year, I walked the neighborhoods and knocked on doors to ask if I could help with any odd jobs.

When classes started in September, I was thrilled to see the campus come alive again. The weather was still warm, I had moved back to the North Tower dormitory, and I was feeling a whole lot more comfortable in my own skin. I had a new roommate, Thomas, who was also a sophomore. His family lived in the upscale North Shore area of Milwaukee.

I discovered something glorious in my sophomore year—money was *not* a prerequisite for hanging out with the girls who attended Eau Claire. It didn't cost anything to walk with them on campus or to lie next to them on a blanket that was spread across soft, green grass. I found Wisconsin girls beautiful, hardy, and fun to be with, and I spent the year making up for all those lost opportunities when I didn't have money or a car. I needed neither to have a social life at Eau Claire. The girls provided the transportation. They'd take me to their favorite bars and hangouts. Several girls took me to their hometowns more than once to visit their parents.

My world began to broaden significantly with these trips off campus. I met hardworking families who practiced values like honesty and truth and perseverance. I saw how a truly loving family works. They welcomed me warmly. Even the fathers treated me well, which meant that I was good enough to date their daughters.

My roommate Thomas invited me for a weekend at his parents' house in Milwaukee. It was deep winter, but by that time I'd acquired a jacket and other warm clothing suitable for Wisconsin's arctic cold.

A compassionate shop owner in downtown Eau Claire had given them to me on credit for seven hundred and fifty dollars. I signed a note promising to pay the money back when I graduated.

Thomas's parents' two-story house was grand: large, sparkling chandeliers hung from the ceilings; the hardwood floors and furniture were polished; beautiful, thick rugs lay in each room; and a Mercedes sedan was parked in the driveway. Everything, inside and out, looked brand-new. I had my own room with a luxurious, thick-mattressed bed; crisp, fine linens; and rich draperies running the full length of the tall windows in my room. This was the first night I'd ever spent in the home of a truly rich family. They welcomed me with extraordinary warmth and kindness without patronizing me. After dinner, Thomas's father took the two of us into his book-lined study and talked about how he had succeeded in life. He talked to me about never giving up on my dreams. "Don't lose your way," he said. "If necessary, go around, under, over, or through any obstacle that gets in your path. If you lose your way, it's because you allowed an obstacle to block you." I learned more in a few days with this man than I'd learned in a lifetime with my father.

CHAPTER THIRTY-FOUR

Gaining Entrance to One Social Class Leaves Another Behind

I n March, Bracy took the bus from Nashville to visit me at school, and once he arrived, he decided to stay for the rest of the semester. I was embarrassed that my brother had not only shown up unannounced, but also that he wanted to share my small dormitory room with me and my roommate. Thomas was generous about it and said Bracy could stay with us. At first, it was awkward because my brother wasn't a student and it violated campus rules for him to stay in the room. But Bracy made friends quickly and soon found himself at home in the campus environment. I was hoping that he would take advantage of being at Eau Claire to do something about his faltering life. We talked about the possibility of him taking the GED and then applying to college. But Bracy was caught up in time-wasting and career-delaying behavior and, I could see, had no real intention or strong-enough desire to continue his education.

Soon, he met two girls, who were not college students, and spent most days and nights at their place. He wasn't working nor did he seek a job. He just hung out with the girls, drank their beer, and generally had a great time. At first, I hung out with the three of them too, but then I started falling behind in my studies, so I stopped. I didn't want to go back to the kind of life that I'd had in Nashville, not even with Bracy. I loved Bracy's company, as I always had, yet this time I was happy when the semester was over and he decided to go back to Nashville.

Bracy's visit was the first of many situations with my brothers in which my drive and ambition created an unspoken wall between us. After Bracy returned to Nashville—though we'd stay loving brothers forever—our relationship was never the same.

During school holidays I often visited my family in Nashville. Since I didn't have the bus fare, I hitched rides the entire nine hundred miles, and over time, I became quite expert at it—even in winter.

My visits home from college were bittersweet. I was thrilled to be with my family, and I loved every moment we spent together. But the stark contrast between my relatively secure life at school and the wretched conditions that persisted within the dismal concrete-block walls of 802 South Seventh Street made me uneasy. The joy of seeing everyone again was laced with anxiety and sorrow and worry. Mom was still working, but there was a constant lack of money. Mom often spoke of her fatigue in her letters: "Because I don't write often is no sign I don't think about you. It's always I'm tired. I had to work all day last Saturday, but I will try my darnedest to write more often." The only change for the better was that my father continued to stay away from the family.

Each time I visited home, I would find a job to help bring in some money. I worked parking cars or, at Christmastime, I worked retail at Harvey's Department Store downtown. I'd keep fifty dollars to take back to school with me and give the rest to Mom. I rarely spoke about my college life to the family, nor did I discuss it with my Nashville friends. It just didn't seem appropriate. As hard as it was moving up from one class to another, it was equally difficult to settle back into the way of life I left behind. Though I loved my family dearly I felt uncomfortable with the social behaviors of the poverty class. I carried an enormous guilt for having escaped that way of life. It was very depressing for me to accept that moving up had created such a social divide between my family and me.

In the fall of 1969 I started my junior year of college. By that time, I felt comfortable both inside and outside the classroom. In many ways, I was still a stranger in a strange land, but now this stranger had friends, male and female. And my grades were high.

Then, everything derailed.

I had signed up to take a speech class. A few weeks in, I realized two things. First, I didn't like the class. Second, and more importantly, I was far too nervous to speak before a group. The prospect of standing up in front of the class terrified me. So I dropped the class, thinking that, still early in the term, there was time to pick up another. I had never dropped a class before, and didn't know that the deadline for schedule changes had passed. There wasn't time to enroll in another class, after all, and having dropped speech, I was no longer classified as a full-time student. In October, I received a notice from the U.S. Army. I had been drafted. I was allowed to finish out the semester, which ended in December.

Once I had come to understand my part-time student status, which I couldn't fix until the start of next term, I'd had a few weeks to mentally prepare myself for this possibility—although I hadn't expected the military to act quite so quickly. It needed bodies, however, and hadn't wasted any time. Admitting to my mistake in dropping the speech class was as devastating as receiving the draft notice. But I had to accept responsibility for both the mistake and its consequences. I had to move on.

CHAPTER THIRTY-FIVE

In the Army

I n December 1969, at the height of the Vietnam War, I was sent to Fort Campbell, Kentucky, for basic training. I arrived at the base with about twelve hundred other inductees, ranging in age from eighteen to twenty-four (I was twenty). We were not a happy group. Fort Campbell was just across the state line from Stewart County, but it might as well have been a thousand miles away. Though I was in close proximity to home, I never left the base. Every aspect of my life became entwined in Fort Campbell. Once the military takes custody of your physical body, it owns everything about you. It controls your time, your space, and your thoughts, and it constantly keeps your mind distracted so that you don't focus too much on yourself.

Basic training lasted for twelve weeks, and by design, it was a test of physical and mental endurance. Our sergeant, for example, made all fifty of us crawl on our bellies in the mud underneath our barracks as punishment when one of us broke the rules. After a few such punishments, we all came down pretty hard on any fellow recruit who violated the rules. It seemed torturous at the time, but I believe that those in charge were just doing their best to harden up the troops and get us mentally and physically prepared to deal with the stress of battle.

For me, lack of sleep was the most difficult aspect of basic training. I was in prime fighting condition. I had fast hands, fast feet, and was physically strong. Often, though, we'd be awakened at 1 a.m. to run ten miles while packing fifty pounds of military gear on our backs. The interruption of sound sleep was far more punishing than the run. Physically, I was solid. Mentally, I struggled with exhaustion.

To graduate from basic training, we had to satisfactorily complete a physically strenuous obstacle course in order to move on to advanced training. If we failed to complete the obstacle course within the required amount of time, we had to repeat the whole twelve weeks of basic training. To avoid this nightmare, we were willing to put up with almost any kind of abuse from the drill sergeants, who freely threatened recycling us back through basic training to motivate us into giving 100 percent.

During the obstacle course examination, the drill instructors rated us using a variety of criteria. The first two soldiers to complete the course received a promotion from E-1 to E-2, which meant a second stripe on the private's uniform. That meant not only an increase in pay, but also a step up in rank from the bottom of the pile. Determined to be one of the top two finishers, I finished first and received both the promotion and the increase of fifty dollars in my monthly pay. I requested that the pay increase be deducted from my check each month and mailed directly to my mother from the U.S. Army in the form of an allotment. This allowed my mother to once again receive reliable monthly revenue checks from the government.

After graduating from basic training, soldiers were assigned a job classification, known as a military occupational skill, or MOS, which essentially defined the type of work the soldier would be doing in the military. That job classification was issued in the form of a written order, which commanded the soldier to report to a specific facility for further training. If the soldier voluntarily enlisted in the military, he had the privilege of choosing the job he wanted. If he'd been drafted, as I was, he was not given a choice and had to accept whatever job was assigned. Routinely, draftees were assigned to the infantry, the soldiers who saw action.

My MOS was identified as 11B, the army code for infantry soldier. I was sent to Fort Polk, Louisiana, for advanced combat training.

Fort Polk was well known within the military as "Little Vietnam." The Louisiana swamps provided a perfect environment for training soldiers for battle in Southeast Asia. Out of the twelve hundred soldiers who trained with me at Fort Campbell, nine hundred of us, dressed in dark-green uniforms, were sent to Fort Polk in a convoy of a dozen chartered buses. We boarded single file and alphabetically by last name. With a name like Wallace, I was always at the back of the line. I remember we were an especially quiet group for the long twelve hours it took to get to Louisiana. The only sound was the rumble of the engine. I think many of us were despondent about the fact that our worst fears had been realized; we'd been drafted and were heading for combat training. Only four months earlier, I'd been in Wisconsin watching war protestors from the window of my college dorm. Now I was a statistic in an army bus, ultimately destined for Vietnam.

A hundred and fifty miles south of Shreveport, our convoy passed through the guarded entrance gates of Fort Polk. It was late, sometime after midnight. There was anxious chattering among the soldiers as the buses quickly came to a stop in a vast, empty parking lot. We pressed our faces against the windows and stared into the darkness, trying to get some idea of where we'd landed and why. Some speculated that we'd stopped in this remote area because we were going to be made to run through the swamps as some sort of physical exercise. Others suggested that the bus driver was lost.

As we all crowded at the windows, a Specialist 5th Class, a rank similar to that of a sergeant, jumped on the bus and shouted, "Everybody off the bus. Fall in line. Now!"

As we exited the bus, I noticed other soldiers from the convoy already lined up in a single file stretching deep into the dark emptiness of the parking lot. I lined up in the formation and stood as directed. Each soldier was holding his own personnel file, known as a 201, containing all his military-related records. The U.S. Army was still years away from having computer files on soldiers, so it was standard procedure that soldiers took their own hard-copy 201 files along with them to every new assignment.

The Specialist 5th Class, together with a lieutenant, worked his way toward my end of the line. Together, they inspected the 201 file of every soldier in the convoy. When they got to me, the lieutenant asked for my file, looked at it briefly, and said, "Fall out, soldier." Promptly, I stepped out of the line. Once everyone's 201 had been given a cursory review, the soldiers were ordered back into the buses—with the exception of those who had been ordered to fall out—six of us altogether. We waited as hundreds of soldiers reboarded the bus convoy, and then watched as it slowly snaked its way out of the parking lot and disappeared into the night. The lieutenant then ordered us to board the rear of a canvas-covered military truck. We had no idea what had happened or where we were going.

The truck traveled only a mile or so on the base and then stopped. It was now about five o'clock in the morning, and we had not slept in more than twenty-four hours. The driver, a civilian employed by the army, handed us an address on the base and told us to report for work there in two days' time, on Monday at 8 a.m.

"Where do we sleep?" I asked.

"There are plenty of empty barracks right here. Just pick one," he shouted as he sped away. We stared after the truck in disbelief.

I felt an immense sense of relief. For the past four months, the military had had absolute control over every aspect of my life. Even though I had no idea what plans the army had in store for me, the fact that I was no longer on that bus was a relief.

After a moment of stunned silence, the six of us introduced ourselves to each other—Paul, Donald, Carl, Justin, James, and myself—and began speculating about why we'd been pulled from the convoy. The only thing that we seemed to have in common was the fact that we had all attended college. Otherwise, we came from different regions of the country and had diverse backgrounds. We also talked about how miserable our comrades on the bus must be at that very moment.

Fort Polk stretched for miles. We'd been dropped off in a section that looked very much like the basic training facility at Fort Campbell, except there were no soldiers to be seen anywhere.

Two-story barracks, each about thirty feet wide and fifty feet long, lined both sides of the street as far as we could see. On the first floor of each barrack were rows of bunk beds, a large private bedroom typically reserved for the drill sergeant, a restroom, and showers. The second floor was a duplicate of the first except for the absence of showers. Our small group spent the first day, without having slept, exploring. We discovered that tens of thousands of soldiers were living on the base. It just so happened that our particular area was unoccupied at the time. Finally, around seven o'clock that evening, we went to bed, thoroughly exhausted. Each of us chose a separate building for our sleeping quarters so that we could each take the private bedroom. It was our first weekend of peace and quiet and freedom since we'd been drafted.

Sunday morning I went to church with the other five guys. The chapel was crowded and we stayed just long enough to say our prayers, with a special prayer of gratitude for our current situation. We spent the remainder of the day trying to find out—without success—why we were isolated from the rest of the base. Sunday night we went to bed just as confused about our status as we had been when we arrived.

I lay in bed for hours, wondering what the future held. Finally, near midnight, I drifted off to sleep. My watch read two when I was awakened by the sound of men rushing into the barracks, their voices and heavy footsteps just outside my bedroom door. It took a moment to realize where I was and to get out of bed to investigate what was going on. The general sleeping area of the barracks was filled with new recruits—they still had their long hair. These guys hadn't even been processed into the system yet. I closed my door and waited for things to calm down, but the noise only grew louder.

Finally, as if I were the drill sergeant, I stormed out of my room wearing only my underwear and shouted, "Listen up, knuckleheads. If I hear one more peep in this room, you guys will be sleeping in the crawl space of this building tonight. Have I made myself clear?" I stared straight ahead and waited for a response. The room was silent. I shouted louder, "Have I made myself clear?"

This time they all replied, "Yes, sir!"

Amused, I returned to my bedroom and, comforted by the silence, fell back to sleep.

The next morning, the recruits stayed clear of me while I showered and got ready for the day. I knew what they were going through and felt sorry for them. New recruits never know what is going on—or who's in charge. Everyone outranks the recruit, so from that perspective it really doesn't matter who is in charge. It is enough to drive a person crazy. You are herded from one place to another, made to stand in long lines, and shouted at all day long. These guys had no idea that I was little more than a recruit myself. And I certainly did not have the authority to make them crawl underneath the barracks— or do anything else for that matter.

I met up with my five compadres and we reported as ordered at eight o'clock to the commanding officer's office. We learned that we'd been pulled from the bus because our 201 files indicated that we had attended college and that we could type. My typing class at Stewart

County High School and my enrollment at Eau Claire were the sole reasons why I was pulled out of line on Friday night.

The Specialist 5th Class, who was also the company clerk, gave us each a typing test to confirm our skills and then put us to work immediately. My job was to assist in processing new recruits into the system. Specifically, I completed the information regarding the Serviceman's Group Life Insurance policy, which paid ten thousand dollars to the beneficiary of the soldier in the event that he was killed on active duty. While at Fort Polk, I processed thousands of guys, spending fewer than ten minutes with each new recruit. I typed in the name of the soldier, his age, the name of the beneficiary, and other personal information.

Even though I was one of them, I felt compassion for many of the guys that I processed, especially those who were obviously intimidated and afraid. Most had been drafted right out of high school. Since they'd arrived, I was among the first military men with whom they could talk one-on-one and, unfortunately, that conversation had to be about a life insurance policy. They were brimming with questions. In particular, every one of them wanted to know whether they were being shipped to Vietnam. Because I was sitting behind a desk, they thought I knew the answer. I didn't have the heart to tell them that being in Fort Polk was a bad omen. They would find out soon enough on their own anyway. More than 80 percent of the guys seated in front of me were destined for Vietnam.

I was an anomaly in Fort Polk—an infantry soldier legally absent from his training. The rules were created to be obeyed and there were not supposed to be any exceptions. The military doesn't deal well with exceptions. The officers in our work area, a large warehouse-like facility, acknowledged that we'd been plucked from the system because of an urgent shortage of typists—the army had drafted more men than it could process. The Specialist 5th Class told us that, technically, he was not our boss. Our next set of orders would be given at the same time that our entire class—the soldiers in the bus convoy—graduated from combat training, in twelve weeks' time.

Once this was explained, it became clear to us how precarious our situation was. The six of us talked over how the army could send us to Vietnam without having trained us for combat. On one hand, we wanted our records to reflect that, as infantry soldiers, we were not receiving the proper training. On the other, we were hesitant to raise the issue for fear that we'd be ordered back to our unit. None of us wanted to be sent to advanced combat training in preparation for Vietnam. For the time being, we decided to lie low.

The clerk position was a fantastic assignment for a guy just graduated from basic training. Our hours were from 8 a.m. to 5 p.m., which would have been unimaginable only a few days before. And for me, my position and status were enhanced by the promotion to E-2, which I had received at Fort Campbell. I was allowed to leave the post at my own leisure and wasn't required to work on weekends. I outranked the other guys taken off the bus with me that night, and I was treated differently by our superiors at work. I made friends among career soldiers on the base and hung out with them at local clubs off-base and took road trips with them to different towns around the area, like Lake Charles. I loved Cajun culture and Cajun girls and was intrigued by the French language spoken in that part of the country.

After two untroubled months, I decided to return my attention to the problem of my job classification. I set up a meeting between the other five clerks and our commanding officer. A meeting with the CO is serious business and you don't go into it without being prepared. We didn't want to register a complaint about having been taken off the bus that night by members of the CO's own staff. Rather, without trying to attach blame, we focused on our situation. We argued that classifying us as combat soldiers was incorrect when our training had been preparing us to be company clerks.

The CO told us that this kind of problem had never happened before within his company and would never happen again. He warned us that if we pressed the issue, we risked being sent back to infantry. His position was basically "Why rock the boat?" Yet, we persisted. We believed our self-interest depended on it. Our infantry class was scheduled for graduation any week. Respectfully, we requested that our orders be revised to reflect our clerical, not combat, training. Any review of the records would reveal that we had been pulled from our primary assignment without proper orders. This and the short time frame seemed to irritate the CO considerably. To fix the problem was going to require paperwork—and paperwork takes personnel time, requires follow-up, and has to be submitted up the chain of command. We left the CO's office unsure of what was going to happen to us.

Soldiers in the clerk's office told us that our meeting had created quite a stir. The lieutenant who had us taken off the bus had been called into the CO's office and questioned about his decision. Suddenly, we were not very popular in the office. Our coworkers wanted very little to do with us. I worried that we might suffer retaliation.

Over the next few weeks, information filtered down and we heard that we were going to be assigned to the next incoming combat class. If there is a certainty in the U.S. Army, it is that there is no certainty.

Then things grew brighter. A member of our group received orders to report to the army recruiting office in downtown St. Louis. His job classification had been changed to that of recruiter. To the remaining five of us, this was auspicious news, indeed. One by one, the other four received orders for recruiter positions in major cities across the country.

I was absolutely thrilled and couldn't wait to receive my own orders. I wondered which city I would be assigned to. I pictured myself wearing my pressed uniform in the recruiter's office in Chicago or New Orleans. A few more days went by and still no word. Finally, three months after arriving at Fort Polk, I received my orders to report to Seattle, Washington. I was not assigned to be a recruiter. My job classification remained infantry.

Upon arriving in Seattle, I was to be flown to a destination referred to as APO SF 96271. I knew this meant overseas, but not exactly where overseas. I walked to the CO's office and asked the Specialist 5th Class to identify the country in my orders. He looked at the destination code. "Um, APO SF 96721—looks like you're going to Vietnam," he said. My worst fears had been realized. I was assigned to Vietnam as a combat soldier—with no combat training.

CHAPTER THIRTY-SIX

Korea

After thirty days' leave in Nashville, I took a Greyhound bus cross-country to Fort Lewis Army Base in Seattle. I had told my family about going to Vietnam, but decided *not* to tell them about my lack of combat training. It would only have caused my mother worry.

The size of a small city, Fort Lewis, situated on Puget Sound, was where soldiers going to and heading back from Asia were sent for processing. Upon reporting, I handed my orders to an army specialist and was pleasantly surprised. My assignment, APO SF 96271, was for Korea—not Vietnam! I felt as though a huge weight had been lifted off my shoulders.

In the few days I was there, I received my immunizations for Korea and met many soldiers on their way to Vietnam. Though I had been oddly calm, I had just spent the past thirty days thinking I was on my way there too, steeling myself for whatever might lie ahead.

The soldiers at Fort Lewis all had the same blank look of resignation. They had cranked up their bravery to get into fighting mode, to prepare for the shock and awe of combat. I felt I could see behind the facade of calm because, until a few hours before, I had worn the same expression. My emotions—the fear of the unknown, of having to kill someone, of being shot at, of dying in a foreign land—had shut down and my body had started going through the motions on its own. I felt enormous compassion for these young boys and men.

As for me and my reprieve, I felt as if I'd just received a stay of execution, as if I'd been saved from plunging off a cliff. The relief was immense.

The flight to Korea took ten hours, the airplane fully loaded with soldiers of all ranks. It was the first time I had ever flown. At that altitude, the clouds and blue spring sky were sublime. Looking out the window, I fell into a reverie on fate and chance. When the U.S. Army had drafted me six months before, I had no doubt that I was intended for the battlefields in Vietnam. I traced events back to the typing class I had taken at Stewart County High School, which wouldn't have happened if I had not been called to Mamma Pearl's as a result of Papa Jim's death. Then, I'd enrolled in college at UW Eau Claire, which wouldn't have happened if I had not dropped out of East Nashville High School and entered the Job Corps. Then, finally, at the army base in Louisiana, I'd been snatched off a military bus in the wee hours of the morning, which wouldn't have happened if there hadn't been an urgent need for typists, preferably with some college. The twists and turns seemed uncannily interconnected.

Were these events mere chance? Were they fate? The intervention of angels? Was free will involved?

I ruled out chance. I believed too much in grace by then, and also the freedom of choice. So far in my young life, at every turning point, however small or large, at every crisis that appeared dire—including the prospect of Vietnam—I could relax my spirit into the mantra-like message I'd been given at age twelve: Everything will be all right. I had infinite faith in the light of these few words, which, when I tapped into them, could take me straight past my circumstances to a profound serenity of peace and safety. From that place of inner knowing, I had the heart to move forward. It was almost as if I were being taken by the hand. And then it was up to me.

CHAPTER THIRTY-SEVEN

A New Cultural Experience

W e touched down in Seoul, where I was temporarily assigned to an army base downtown. My first order of business was to address the issue of my job classification with the company clerk. All problems in the U.S. Army ultimately go through the company clerk's desk. I told him that even though I was classified as infantry, I had had no formal combat training. He reviewed my 201 file and laughed at the idea of a soldier standing on the 38th parallel border with North Korea and holding an M16 rifle that he had never been trained to shoot. In 1953, North Korea had agreed to a truce that ended hostilities with the United States, but had not signed a peace treaty. Until North Korea signed the treaty, the war was not officially over. So, from a military point of view, North Korea was still considered a combat zone, where the *potential* for combat existed.

The company clerk agreed that it would be a mistake to assign me to infantry as instructed by my orders. He promised to discuss the issue with his CO. A few days later, I was on my way to Camp Humphreys, an army installation thirty-five miles south of Seoul on the west coast of South Korea. My job assignment had been changed to company clerk, for which I was relieved and grateful. My official classification still read "combat soldier," however, which nagged at me.

The jeep ride from Seoul down Highway 1 took us through green farmland and rolling hills with the shadowy silhouette of a long mountain range in the distance. Rice paddies lined either side of the road, and men, women, and children all wearing straw hats labored in the fields. Clusters of grass huts dotted the landscape. My driver was a soldier from Iowa who was nicknamed Crow because he could imitate a rooster's crow with perfection.

Just before entering the main gate at Camp Humphreys, we drove through the tiny village of Anjung-ri, which lay immediately adjacent to the base. Housing far worse than that in any American slum I had ever seen crowded Anjung-ri's few treeless, unpaved streets. Both sides of the main road were crowded with sleazy bars and lounges that catered specifically to GIs. Teenage Korean girls, obviously prostitutes, slouched in doorways. Except for pony- and ox-carts, our jeep was the only vehicle in sight. Korean merchants and residents stared as we drove by. Naked children trailed behind us shouting, "Hello, GI! Hello, GI!"

At headquarters I was briefed on the nature of Camp Humphreys's activities. We were the 19th Support Brigade. The base provided direct support for all of South Korea and also served as a storage depot for all of the army's conventional ammunition in Korea. I was assigned to the 19th Aviation Company, an assault support helicopter unit. The base, built in 1941, had been used in both World War II and the Korean War, during which it was known as K-6. The camp's main feature was, and still is, its airstrip, which runs nearly the entire length of the base and is the largest and busiest military airfield outside of the United States.

Since my assignment had placed me in the CO's office, the first thing I did was request the CO sign an order changing my job classification from trained infantry soldier to company clerk, which he did. I then submitted the signed document to headquarters in Seoul and, six weeks later, received notice that the orders had been approved. At last, my job training and job classification were in alignment.

Camp Humphreys was a huge, flat, sparse expanse of land. The original Quonset huts from World War II were still standing. The CO's office, where I worked, was situated in the middle of the camp in a large concrete-block building painted light gray. Beautiful, it was not. At the time, big as it was, the base was lightly populated so it was generally quiet, which suited me fine. Soldiers complained of boredom, but I never found that to be a problem. I was ever mindful of what the alternative might have been for me.

Four other company clerks—all college graduates—served in the CO's office with me, along with several commissioned officers. The primary function of the 19th Aviation Company was to transport troops and ammunition to and from the combat zone in the event of open hostilities from North Korea. The company maintained a variety of helicopters, including the Chinook, the largest military helicopter, each one capable of transporting thirty-seven troops and major supplies to wherever they were needed. The 19th was the only army helicopter unit in Korea and included some of the U.S. Army's finest soldiers. I was honored to be associated with this elite group.

As company clerks, working 8 a.m. to 5 p.m., Monday through Friday, we took care of the Mount Everest of paperwork involved in the day-to-day operations of the company. This included communications with Internal Affairs, the Pentagon, Congress, and the Central Intelligence Agency. Our job was a lot like the character Radar O'Reilly in the hit TV series *M*A*S*H*. We fielded every kind of question from soldiers on the base. The top ten were:

How does one get permission to travel off-base?
What is the procedure for sending money home?

How does one obtain an emergency leave to the States?
Who does one talk to in order to file a complaint?
How does one change a job classification?
What is the procedure for going on a religious retreat?
How does one get permission to see a doctor?
What is the penalty for violation of the regulations?
What is the process to marry a Korean girl?
What is the procedure for handling conflicts between soldiers?

As a company clerk, if you're doing your job properly, you have to be able to answer questions like these on the spot, which means becoming familiar with the army's tomes of rules and regulations. Rules and regulations exist for every conceivable circumstance and, unless an individual is familiar with all of them, there's no way that one man can make a final decision.

To make it as easy as possible, the clerks produced an index of frequently asked questions as an aid to help us respond quickly and accurately. For example, the question of how to marry a Korean citizen came up surprisingly often. The army did everything possible to give a soldier a chance to think carefully before rushing into marriage, so the whole process took from six months to a year. Only after the completion of the paperwork, which could fill an entire file drawer, and permission from the CO, was a soldier permitted to marry someone who was not a U.S. citizen.

Camp Humphreys operated the only military jail in Korea. When soldiers got into legal trouble, on-base or off-base, I was responsible for the paperwork, which was a significant part of my job. The documentation for a court martial was lengthy and had to be error free. Though it was time consuming, I was just glad to be on the right side of the typewriter.

Our sleeping quarters were located in the same large building where I worked. In fact, my bunk was only twenty feet from my office. A thick concrete wall separated the two. In addition to the CO's operation, the building also housed the mailroom, a lounge, a restroom with twenty showers, and enough bunk beds, sectioned off in groups of six, to accommodate seventy-five soldiers. Each barracks was required to have a certain number of Korean soldiers as a way of encouraging the U.S. and South Korean armies to work together. Our building housed about twenty.

The Koreans were known as KATUSA soldiers, which my Korean soldier friends would say was an acronym for Korean Army Tigers/United States Army. However, KATUSA soldiers were not, strictly speaking, Korean Army Tigers. Korean Tigers were soldiers who'd served in Vietnam and who were reputed to be fearless combatants. The North Vietnamese were supposedly terrified of the Tigers. When Korean Tigers swept through enemy territory, it was said, they left few survivors. Supposedly the Vietcong would retreat at the first sign of them. Such stories were repeated often during my stay in Korea.

I became good friends with a number of the Korean soldiers on the base. One of these friends, Kim, from my barracks, explained to me that all Korean men were required to perform military service and that KATUSA was considered to be the choice assignment. Many of the wealthy and influential Korean families would "arrange" to have their sons serve with the Americans as KATUSA soldiers. The other option was the Korean Army, in which the training was supposedly rigorous and brutal, and the officers' treatment of the soldiers was less regulated than in the U.S. military.

On weekends, I traveled the countryside as much as I could, with my KATUSA friends as tour guides. They gave me a rare inside view of Korean culture, including inside their own village homes where I saw family life unlike anything I had known or imagined. For example, extended families—husbands, wives, children, aunts, uncles, grandparents—all might live under the same roof. Usually, one room of the compound was set aside as a shrine to the Buddha. The rooms of the compound surrounded a dirt or stone central courtyard. The outer entrance was a gate of heavy wooden or metal double doors, the inner entrance a sliding door of rice paper and light wood, much like the *shoji* screens in Japanese architecture. Each room inside the compound also had similar rice-paper doors. The ceilings were no more than six feet high and were supported by intricately carved wooden beams, so at six feet tall, I had to remain hunched over when I was inside. Often, when visiting, I was invited to a meal for which we sat cross-legged on straw mats on the floor. Usually, the meal included a ramen soup made with fiery Korean spices.

Although less often, I also spent time in the cities of Seoul and Taegu, a seaside town at the southernmost point of the country. One weekend, Kim, my best Korean friend, invited me to his family's penthouse apartment in Seoul. He told me, as we drove the thirty-five miles north, that I would meet his younger adoptive mother. His biological mother lived in Taegu. His father, who I learned had two wives, was away on business and wouldn't be home.

Unlike anything I'd seen in the villages, Kim's city apartment was spacious and elegant, with beautiful painted screens, tall ceilings, and polished hardwood walls and floors. True to his culture, Kim considered my visit an honor, so he'd invited some of his female Korean friends, university students, to join us that evening for the occasion. None of these young women spoke English and I think they were as curious about meeting an American as I was about meeting them. After exploring the city for a while, we all returned to the apartment. We sat on the penthouse balcony, eighteen floors up, overlooking the lights of downtown Seoul and talking, with Kim as translator, until dawn, when we said good-bye to the girls and finally went to bed. Without a word, Kim's adoptive mother came quietly into my room and placed a tray of ice water and a hot towel next to the bed. Immediately, I fell into a deep sleep, not awakening until two in the afternoon, when Kim's mother mysteriously appeared again with a fresh glass of water.

Camp Humphreys had a good library, and I spent a lot of time reading while I was there. The army library in Seoul was even better, so I could order a book and have it within a day or two. The base was the perfect environment for reading and the guys who I worked with were avid readers, too. We regularly exchanged books. I remember reading biographies of Beethoven and Einstein and loving the novel *Giles Goat Boy* by John Barth. Normally, soldiers have little time to read when doing duty overseas, but being in Korea was like being on vacation. We had Korean house servants, all boys and men, who made our beds exactly as required by the military—even better. They washed and dried our clothes, starched our shirts and pants, and then ironed them. They cleaned all the common rooms in the barracks. They waxed and polished the floors, shined our shoes, rolled our socks and placed them in our lockers neatly, military-style. Submitting to routine inspection was a joke. The CO checks your bunk, locker, and uniform, looking for anything untidy or awry—something not cleaned, folded, rolled, ironed, shined, or stored exactly according to regulation. But with the help we were getting, everything was—at all times—top-shelf, no-dust.

"Who is he inspecting—the house servant?" we joked.

Each soldier in the barracks paid each house servant—there might be four or five in a single barracks—fifty cents a week. The only thing the servants didn't do was our primary assignments. Relieved of some of our duties, we had plenty of time for reading.

I once asked the CO why so many house servants were on base, including servants for the privates. He said he didn't know, but that they had been there from day one.

I asked the house servant who hired him. "You did, GI," he said.

According to rumor, one of the commanders had once tried to get rid of the servants by refusing them entrance to the base. They were enraged. A riot became a real possibility, along with the threat of buildings being set on fire. Thereafter, so the story went, no CO ever tried to do away with the house servants again.

The truth was that the entire town of Anjung-ri was dependent upon Camp Humphreys for its economic survival.

One Saturday, soon after arriving on the base, I was sitting outside in the sun reading a book when I noticed a group of about twenty soldiers, all wearing white martial arts uniforms with belts of varying colors, running by barefoot on the hot asphalt road. The scene took me back to summers in Tennessee running barefoot on the gravel roads as a boy. These guys looked disciplined, formidable, and focused, and it was obvious they were in training. The soldiers seemed to be having a good time together and, immediately, I wanted to be part of that. I got up and followed them. They were training in the Korean martial art of Tae Kwon Do in the empty barracks on the base.

The thirty-eight-year-old instructor, Master Kim, had a black belt in the 8th degree, the highest rank. That very day, I enrolled in the class. We practiced every day without fail—for two hours after work on weekdays and four hours on weekends. On weekdays, practice consisted of an hour of instruction, and an hour of sparring. The sparring matches were intense, with fast, high-spinning kicks, defensive blocks, and strategic punches to the body. All over, my body was constantly bruised.

Master Kim was the highest ranking Tae Kwon Do master in Korea. His entire life was dedicated to his art. He bore thick calluses on his forehead, forearms, shins, heels, ankles, and on the balls of his feet. He constantly challenged himself. One day he instructed eight of his students, including me, to separate into two rows of four, facing each other, and each hold a letter-size sheet of ordinary paper in their hands at chest height. He pierced two of these sheets with either end of a four-foot-long wooden stick, suspending it in the air. He did the same thing with three other identical wooden sticks. He then instructed the students to position the four suspended sticks into a perfect square surrounding him. After a moment of complete silence, he jumped straight up, breaking two of the sticks with his feet as he rose from the floor, and breaking the other two sticks on his way down. Not one of the thin sheets of paper was torn. Master Kim's artful jump took him beautifully higher than my six-feet height.

Tae Kwon Do took me to levels far beyond the fighting I'd known. Up until then, I had practiced only one style of fighting—the use of strong, fast hands. Tae Kwon Do involved fast hands, plus the use of legs, hips, elbows, forehead, forearms, and all parts of the feet. My lifetime of fighting was nothing when compared to the fighting skills required of Tae Kwon Do. It was like learning how to fight all over again.

I loved learning how to move my body in ways I didn't know were possible, and how to synchronize my body with my mind, which Master Kim also taught us. Like karate or judo, Tae Kwon Do is a martial art as well as a philosophy, the philosophy of the peaceful warrior. The moves of Tae Kwon Do, when performed by a master, are extraordinary to watch. But for a student to use Tae Kwon Do as a means of showing off was cause for immediate expulsion from Master Kim's class.

Master Kim promoted a peaceful mind through self-discipline and the art of self-mastery. As his students, we pledged a solemn allegiance to commit our knowledge of Tae Kwon Do to improve our own lives and the lives of others around us. We took an oath that applied to our behavior both inside and outside the *dojang,* or training hall:

> *I shall observe the philosophy of Tae Kwon Do.*
> *I shall respect and value our teachers and elders.*
> *I shall never mistreat others or misuse Tae Kwon Do.*

I shall be a champion of freedom and justice.
I shall strive to build a more peaceful world.

I trained daily in Tae Kwon Do for thirteen of my fourteen months in Korea and finished with a brown belt, one step away from the first ranking of black belt.

In the tradition of Tae Kwon Do, brown represents the advanced student whose techniques are beginning to mature.

CHAPTER THIRTY-EIGHT

An Army Divided

During my tour of duty in Korea, I turned twenty-one. A few months before my birthday we got word that the Ohio National Guard had shot and killed four students at Kent State University during a protest against the bombings in Cambodia. Eight million students back in the States went on strike as a consequence of what many were calling the Kent State Massacre. Universities, colleges, and high schools across the country closed.

News like this flowed constantly from home and lowered the morale on the base, including my own, whether you were for or against the war. It was the source of many heated disagreements. Drafted soldiers usually opposed the war in Vietnam; volunteer soldiers usually supported it. The U.S. Congress authorized the Vietnam War without ever having signed an official declaration of war. In my mind, this authorization turned it into a political war, which resulted in no united support for the war and the troops, and no true military strategy for winning.

The other continuous heat on the post was racial. A lot of American soldiers were dying in Vietnam and a large percentage of the soldiers fighting the war were black. Black soldiers believed they were being used inordinately more in combat than white soldiers, who had first dibs on the safer, noncombat positions available. The black soldiers in Korea felt solidarity with their brothers in Vietnam, and only the officers in charge at Camp Humphreys seemed oblivious to the brooding tension on our base. Outside the officer ranks, not one soldier in our brigade was unaware that the black soldiers were unhappy and beginning to direct their anger at the white soldiers.

Three weeks before I was scheduled to go home, things began to spiral out of control. It all started with a hornet's nest of rumors—the rumor that the Vietnam War was a tool being used by the United States to kill off black soldiers, the rumor that Korean shops were charging higher prices to black soldiers than white soldiers, the rumor that Korean prostitutes were asking twice their normal fees of blacks. It was the last that ignited the powder keg.

One Friday night, in a neon-lit club in Anjung-ri, I was sitting at a table with an American nurse named Judy from the base. The Korean club owner suddenly rushed over and directed us to follow him to the back. Seeing his panic, I scanned the room and saw at the club entrance six black soldiers standing at parade rest, the military position of feet shoulder-width apart, face forward, and hands clasped firmly behind the back. Customers were hurrying out. In seconds, the soldiers blocked the exit, no longer allowing anyone else to leave. Dozens of black soldiers poured into the bar and began beating up on white soldiers who'd remained inside. They threw chairs and generally began trashing the place. I grabbed Judy's arm and we followed the Korean owner into a private office. Once inside, he pointed us to a wooden ladder leading to the roof. As we climbed up, we heard the office door close and lock behind us.

Judy and I found ourselves in the open night air on top of the club's clay tile roof, its pitch fortunately slight. The melee had spilled outside of the club, and we crouched down and watched the scene unfold. Black soldiers ran up and down the main street smashing storefront windows. In an alleyway within our view, a group of black soldiers were beating up a lone white soldier. The sounds of fighting came from all around us.

To me, it was obvious this had been an organized assault involving two or three hundred black soldiers. They shouted instructions and pointed boldly in the direction of white soldiers trying to escape. Judy and I decided to stay on the roof. I knew I'd been spared the carnage only because I happened to be with an American girl—one of only two on the post. Wanting to rescue her, the club owner had shown us the secret escape route.

The fighting had lasted for no more than twenty minutes, when things shifted. Hundreds of Korean men carrying sticks, stones, and farm tools swarmed into the streets to defend their village and ran wildly in pursuit of the black soldiers. The entire village was in turmoil. We stayed put for an hour or more, until the club owner retrieved us from the roof and told us it was safe to return to the post. He assured us we wouldn't be harmed as long as we didn't interfere.

Back on the ground, we saw close-up the extensive damage to the businesses and shops on both sides of the dusty road leading to the camp gate. In the darkness, horrifically, we could see a dozen black soldiers buried in the ground with only their battered heads showing. They were alive, but bruised and beaten, and surrounded by a crowd of villagers. The punishment was so brutal, I wondered if any of the village men had been former Korean Tigers in Vietnam. Instinctively, I wanted to help, but I knew my primary responsibility lay in escorting Judy safely back to the base. I held her hand tightly and we walked fast, choosing not to run for fear of being chased.

The next morning, the post was in complete disarray. Our commanders stayed in meetings all day, as if that would solve the problem. Late in the afternoon, all soldiers were called into formation and told that no one would be permitted off-base until further notice.

In Anjung-ri all the bars had been closed indefinitely. A fresh rumor surfaced that another riot was planned. That night, I went to the NCO Club on base. Having achieved the rank of E-5, or Specialist 5th Class, I was now admitted to the club, a nice place reserved for non-commissioned officers.

Around eight o'clock we heard the sound of grenades exploding on the post. We all ran outside the club to see what was going on. Most of us set out for our barracks on the double. As I ran toward mine, another grenade exploded about a hundred yards from me. I dropped to the ground, looked all around and, seeing no one, low-crawled the last fifty yards to my building and my bunk. Widespread panic and pandemonium ensued, with M16 gunfire and grenades going off on the base until dawn. It sounded like a battlefield. I had no weapon, the post was out of control, and I genuinely feared for my life. Needless to say, I didn't sleep that night.

Just before dawn, I heard the rumble of truck convoys, followed by shouts of orders and the footsteps of marching platoons. When it got light, I went outside and found that several hundred U.S. Marines were patrolling the base. They were dressed in full combat gear and armed with M16 rifles. There was no doubt about who was in charge. In part, I found it humorous that the marines were protecting us from ourselves. But mostly, I felt embarrassed as a soldier. If this was what was happening in the military, how could we ever hope to win a war?

Base commanders at all levels were summoned immediately to Seoul headquarters by the top tier of the chain of command, leaving the base under a captain's charge. From what I could see as company clerk, no one in command seemed interested in the root cause of the chaos. Point, blame, and deny knowledge was to be the strategic response to what had happened. Empty investigations, finger-pointing, lies, and mountains of meaningless paperwork lay ahead. Because of the way the situation was handled, I lost respect for all but a handful of those in authority.

That same day I learned that my good friend Bellamy, a black belt in Tae Kwon Do, had been attacked during the riot in Anjung-ri and had been helicoptered to an intensive care unit in a Seoul hospital. Because he was the highest-ranking black belt on the post, I suspected that he'd been specially targeted. His jaw had been broken in two places and he had multiple breaks to his legs, arms, and spine. I wanted to visit him, but we were in complete lockdown—no one was allowed to leave or enter the base.

I became worried that my scheduled departure from Korea was in jeopardy because of the crisis. Thankfully, however, my orders arrived on the third day after the riot. I was scheduled to fly home in less than a week. I had already trained my replacement and was anxious to leave the base before another incident prevented that from happening. The next day I called one of my superior officers, a captain and also a friend, and asked for a seat on the next helicopter leaving for Seoul. He said that he would fly me to Seoul himself. I think he wanted out of there as much as I did. That same afternoon, we flew out in a Huey helicopter. My last image of Camp Humphreys was a bird's-eye view of a camp under siege. I had managed to make it through my time overseas without seeing combat—almost.

My flight from Korea back to the States was on a large commercial jet chartered by the U.S. military. It was a full flight, packed with celebrating soldiers. I had a window seat and spent most of the trip staring out the window at the clear, summer sky. The guys around me were laughing and talking about their wives or girlfriends. There was a lot of giddiness in the air. I remember one guy shouting that when he got home he hoped to never see another soldier for the rest of his life. He laughed and said, "From now on it's football games and cold beer for me."

When the plane touched down in Seattle, I had exactly 179 days remaining in my two-year commitment to the U.S. Army. Having been a student of the army's rules and regulations for the past year, I had discovered an early discharge provision for any soldier who completes a tour of duty in either Vietnam or Korea. There was only one stipulation. The soldier must have less than six months remaining in service on the day that he returns to U.S. soil. One hundred and seventy-nine days was exactly one day under six months.

When all was said and done, I had served a year and a half in the army and obtained an early release for the final six months.

The early release program was a huge benefit—little advertised— and entitled a soldier to a full and complete honorable discharge. I was among the lucky few who landed in Seattle and were allowed to go home for good. I was honorably discharged on July 7, 1971, with the rank of Specialist 5th Class—the equivalent of sergeant in the infantry. Achieving a rank of E-5, especially in such a short time, was an achievement I was proud of.

PART IV

Law Bound

CHAPTER THIRTY-NINE

A Need for Structure

One last flight, from Seattle to Nashville, and I was back home. I had both hopes and misgivings about returning home. My priority remained the same as it had been since third grade, to get my college degree and then to enter law school. To finish my undergraduate work, I planned to enroll in the University of Tennessee that had a campus in downtown Nashville. But I knew deciding to continue my education at home, rather than in Wisconsin, meant re-exposure to the uncertainty and violence of East Nashville, where all of my family was still living. The idea of moving from the structured, disciplined organization of the army to a city in which I had known nothing but trouble cast a shadow of doubt upon my plans.

I was looking forward to seeing my family, but also scared. I felt that I was returning home a completely different person, but from my visits during college and from the letters I'd been getting since I'd been drafted, I knew that not much had changed in the lives of my family. My brothers Bracy, Steve, and Rick were still caught in the web of poverty. Bracy, twenty-four, had married, worked sporadically at minimum wage jobs, and become dependent on alcohol, which seemed to exacerbate every problem in his life. Steve, nineteen, had graduated from East Nashville High School—he would be the only one of us to do so—but had made no plans beyond working odd jobs. He and Bracy had become drinking buddies and I could see nothing good coming out of that. Rick, sixteen, was holding onto high school by his fingernails.

With all these thoughts racing through my mind, my heart began to pound when I saw the familiar Nashville skyline as my plane approached the runway. Once outside I nabbed a taxi and gave the driver my mother's address on Morrow Road in East Nashville. One important thing that *had* changed for the better was that Mom had moved away from the projects to a rental house. This was still a low-rent property, but anything away from South Seventh Street was a step up, however small.

As the taxi pulled into the driveway, I got my first glimpse of Mom's new place. It was a rundown, one-story house in need of paint, but the neighborhood was better than the projects. Any neighborhood in East Nashville was better than the projects.

As I stepped out of the taxi, I became suddenly aware of my uniform and that neither my mother nor anyone else in the family had seen me dressed as a soldier. On my chest were the medals that I had earned and on my shoulders I proudly displayed the E-5 rank that I had achieved. Just then, Mom ran out of the house and embraced me, excited and weeping, in the front yard. We hadn't seen each other in nearly two years.

Four of my brothers were still living at home: Steve and Rick, and then Brady, who was eleven, and Tim, who was eight. Like Faye, my younger sister Donna had dropped out of high school and gotten married. Mom was still working at the Davis Cabinet Company for minimum wage, which had gone up to $1.60 an hour—sixty dollars a week—and her face was still worn from worry and stress. Early every morning—through rain, snow, sleet, hail, severe cold, and sweltering heat—she walked to the bus stop and went to work on the assembly line. She had been working since she was six years old and strong enough to lift a hoe in her father's tobacco fields. Yet she never complained. I told Mom that I planned on getting a job and would continue to help support the family. I promised her that the future would be brighter, that I planned one day to buy her a home that no one could ever take away from her. She smiled and hugged me, but who could find fault if she harbored some doubt in that promise? All she'd ever known was hardship.

A few days later, I began to look for full-time work and applied for fall admission to the University of Tennessee. I had decided to work during the day and attend school at night. While in Korea, I had dreamed of having my own place. I needed a steady flow of income to do that and support myself and also to help support Mom. I could have returned to the University of Wisconsin, but, for me, that was no longer a desirable option. I was no longer the desperate boy striving for a high school diploma and trying to fit in on campus. In four years I had gone from a high school dropout to a college junior and fulfilled a tour of duty overseas in the military. I had become a confident and accomplished man and was ready to take on more responsibility.

I entered into discussions with an old friend, Andy, about the possibility of joining his company. He had opened a rental car business in a prime location in downtown Nashville, close to the Hermitage Hotel, a luxury hotel that at one time was the home of Minnesota Fats. I had known this friend from when I was parking cars downtown and he was driving his own cab. He was in his early thirties and weighed three hundred and fifty pounds, give or take. To try to get his weight under control, he took medication, which seemed to exacerbate a problem he had with managing his anger. He'd yell at his employees, as well as customers. These rants, he acknowledged, were contributing to difficulties he was having in his business. He pleaded with me to work in his front office and deal with the customers. In return, he offered a junior partnership. When I hesitated, he asked me to give it a try for a few weeks. I agreed to thirty days at a salary of a thousand dollars. By the end of the month, I was disenchanted with the rental car business and my friend had proved to be such a horrible business owner—and equally terrible partner—that I walked away. Lesson learned: pick your field of business and your partners carefully.

In late July, I learned that I had been accepted to Tennessee State for the fall semester. I had a month remaining before the start of school. While I was in Korea, a friend from Wisconsin had written to me and proposed a three-week-long road trip, driving the old Route 66, to California. I took him up on the idea. Out of the thousand dollars I'd just made, I left four hundred for Mom, invited my brother Steve to come along, and the three of us set out on a hot summer day for the West Coast in Jeff's '64 Plymouth station wagon. It was a twenty-one-day trip that took us to Los Angeles, Yosemite, Reno, and then back through Wisconsin before we finally headed back to Nashville.

The day after we returned to Nashville, I went to a professional recruiting firm downtown. I made it clear that I would only consider jobs for which the employer paid the recruiter's fees. The military had enhanced my self-image and made me a stronger person. I was smarter, better, and faster in every way. I had learned to work in a team, with a healthy dose of competition in the mix. As company clerk I had acquired new administrative skills. In my final two months in Korea, I was the top-ranking soldier in the CO's office, with top-secret security clearance, in charge of all company clerks. I felt confident that I could handle any task a civilian employer could throw at me.

On my first interview, I was offered a job as a debt adjustor by the Frost Arnett Company, the parent corporation for a large credit bureau and debt management firm. Their offices were located in the Stahlman Building in the town center. The job involved contacting delinquent customers, both individuals and companies, by telephone and assisting them with a plan to work out the past due amount. It seemed to be a perfect day job for a student attending college at night, a job that involved little stress. The pay was twelve thousand dollars a year, the same salary I would have earned at my friend's car rental agency.

The owner of the company, Charles C. Martin, a man in his late sixties, had been in the business of debt management since he was my age. He'd purchased Frost Arnett from the founders, who had suffered great losses during the Depression and were selling the company for a good price. Mr. Martin was by all measures a very rich man. For me, working for him was an opportunity to learn from a highly successful entrepreneur, a perfect complement to the business courses I was taking at college. I accepted the job and signed a contract for a period of no less than six months.

On my first day, I learned that Frost Arnett was no ordinary workplace, and that Mr. Martin was no ordinary business owner. The company occupied several floors of the historic Stahlman Building— a twelve-story, Beaux Arts–style building located on Union Street, a few blocks from the river. Except for corner offices, each floor was a big open area, with rows and rows of identical, perfectly aligned wooden desks. Sitting behind each desk was a clean-shaven white male with short hair. There were no female adjustors; the only female employees were clerical assistants.

Mr. Martin managed every detail of the office. He required all male employees to wear a crisp white shirt and conservative tie, and all female employees to wear a dress or skirt. And all employees were expected to purchase and use a fountain pen, filled with black ink only. The top of every desk had to be arranged identically. In the center was a brown leather desk pad, thirty inches wide, which held an absorbent blotter to be changed regularly. Soiled blotters were a no-no. To the right of the desk pad, six inches from the top left desk corner, sat the "call-back" tray and the in-box. To the left was the "left-message-to-call" tray. A black telephone sat on the right. Personal paraphernalia was not allowed on the desk, not even a family photograph. Paper clips, pencils, erasers, staplers, and staple removers all had their assigned place, and each employee was responsible for policing the immediate floor area around his or her desk. Any stray paper clip falling to the floor was to be picked up promptly and put back with the other paper clips. Personal conversations during work hours were strictly forbidden. No one even dared to look up as I was led through the office during my orientation tour. The atmosphere of intimidation was like boot camp and the obsessive precision reminded me of the military in general. This was going to be interesting.

I was trained on the job by a guy named Larry. He seemed to enjoy his status as one of Mr. Martin's favorite employees, but he was odd. He had great communication skills that enabled him to do well on the telephone, but I got the feeling that his life outside the office was a wreck. About my height and thin, he was in his mid- to late thirties and already losing his hair. Larry was, in fact, a practiced office clown, but he was very good at hiding that from the boss. He seemed to take great pleasure in sucking up to Mr. Martin while in his presence, then acting the clown whenever his back was turned.

During training I had to sit in a chair beside Larry's desk and listen on an extension phone to his conversations with customers. After finishing a call, Larry would explain the strategy behind certain words, voice inflections, and rebuttals he had used. At night, for homework, he had me reading training manuals dealing with all aspects of debt management.

Once I had gone through training, I was assigned to my own desk, which was directly outside Mr. Martin's office. Another new employee might think this incredibly bad luck, to be positioned within a few feet of the master of the office universe, but I considered it a good omen to be in such daily, close proximity to the owner of the company. Instinctively, I knew there was opportunity in a tight organization like this for someone who could keep his cool, learn the rules, and then make the rules work for him. In the army, that had been my strategy and it had worked for me.

I found a one-bedroom apartment downtown and signed a year's lease for seven hundred and fifty dollars a month at the Capitol Towers Apartments on the James Robertson Parkway, which was a prime location. The apartment was within easy walking distance of both school and work, which made me quite happy. And having my own place was a milestone for me. Mom was disappointed that I wouldn't be living in her house, but she understood. I would remain a reliable source of support, but I needed the security and privacy of my own place. I needed structure.

Steve landed a steady job as a truck driver for one of the industrial warehouses downtown, and we became roommates, splitting expenses equally. I'd persuaded him to apply for admission to the university, and to attend school at night.

Steve and I were close. We had written letters back and forth ever since I went away to Mamma Pearl's in high school, and then all through my time in Wisconsin and Korea. I had high hopes for him. I thought at the time, wrongly, as it turned out, that I could assist Steve in learning the rules of the middle class by removing him from the bad influences of the East Nashville neighborhoods.

From our north-facing windows and balcony on the fourteenth floor, we had a great view of the Cumberland River, parts of downtown, and the L&N—the Louisville and Nashville—railroad yard. The apartment was unfurnished, so a few days after securing the lease, I went shopping and found a blowout new-furniture sale. I got a complete living room set—couch, loveseat, chair, end tables, coffee table, and lamps—all for the bargain price of four hundred and fifty dollars. Permanent things. I also bought a bedroom set—two single beds with headboards, mattresses, box springs, bedside tables, and a bureau—for an additional three hundred.

I purchased the furniture on credit, but I didn't like the thought of going into debt. I created a plan, right then and there, for paying back the loan in affordable installments over three years. I was keenly aware that being in chronic debt eroded one's self-esteem, and I wanted no part of that. One of the first things I did after finding full-time work was pay back the shop owner in Eau Claire, Wisconsin, who'd trusted me with seven hundred and fifty dollars' worth of winter clothes.

My schedule—working full-time during the day and attending college at night—was brutal. I was in the classroom until ten o'clock, Monday through Friday, and after class studied late into the night. Then work started at eight o'clock in the morning, which meant that I was getting very little sleep. On weekends I drove Mom for her weekly grocery shopping at the farmer's market, where I also worked on Saturday and Sunday nights as a stock clerk. To maintain passing grades, I had to study a minimum of two hours every night, and sometimes four on both Saturday and Sunday.

When I took my mother to the market, I generally paid for all or part of the groceries. If her electricity was going to be turned off or if she was threatened with eviction, I would give her whatever it took to solve the emergency. In our family there was always a crisis. But now that I was living on my own, it was a constant struggle to maintain my independence while ensuring that my mother had whatever she needed to survive. I had to make the conscious decision to exercise discipline when it came to giving money to my family, whose financial needs were beyond my ability to satisfy. I knew the right choice, my first obligation, was to move my career forward and become a lawyer. I had seen how living apart from my family had been in my best interest—and theirs. I would be of no use to them at all if I didn't keep a laser-like focus on my first responsibility, which was to take care of myself. Roughly, my priorities were these, in this order: remain in school, take care of my rent and basic needs, help Mom, receive rapid promotion in my job, and keep my eye on the prize—entering law school. Staying close to my higher power and keeping my independence were prerequisites for all of the above. That inner voice that was telling me everything would be all right had never—*has* never—left me, or let me down.

CHAPTER FORTY

One of Those Handy Skills You Never Want to Use

Near our apartment was the Broadway Barn, a popular nightclub located in downtown Nashville on Music Row. The club had a disc jockey who stood in a sound booth and played rock 'n' roll. One cool October night in the Broadway Barn, I encountered my first trouble since coming home.

I had just entered the club when I spotted a friend from East Nashville standing at the bar. The club was packed with young people, the dance floor crowded, and the music loud. Steve and Rick were in the club seated at a table with several guys they knew from South Seventh Street.

I stopped to talk with my friend at the bar, who said to me straight off, "I think your brother's in trouble."

I turned and saw Steve sandwiched between two large guys in their thirties on the edge of the dance floor. The three of them were arguing. I rushed over and placed myself between these guys and Steve.

"We don't want any trouble here," I said.

I grabbed Steve and led him over to the bar where I had been standing.

"They're rednecks," my brother said. Apparently, from the moment he'd walked into the club, they'd been teasing him about his long hair. The scuffle had started when one of the two asked Steve to dance because his long hair offended them. This deliberate insult had resulted in the argument I'd just interrupted.

I urged Steve to stay away from those guys and suggested we get Rick and leave the nightclub immediately. Before we reached the exit, the same two guys—joined by three others—blocked our path.

They were dressed as though they'd been working at a construction site. They wore faded, mud-stained blue jeans and sleeveless T-shirts that exposed their bulging biceps. Their faces were unshaven and dirty. They were an intimidating lot. Physically, each one of them was larger than any one of us. I could tell they were serious about preventing us from leaving.

I held up my hands with open palms in a gesture of submission and said, "Please, guys, we want no trouble."

Without uttering a word, they slowly took calculated steps toward us, their hands in their pockets. Their attitude suggested a conviction that they could have their way with us and there was absolutely nothing we could do about it.

I repeated my message: "Listen, if you let us walk out that door, there'll be no trouble."

We had no way out and they knew it. Behind us stood the bar. In front of us loomed the human wall created by the five goons. My eyes were fixed on them, while the Rolling Stones' "Brown Sugar" pumped through the club's loudspeakers and couples filled the dance floor. People were laughing and talking all around us, completely oblivious to the threat facing my brothers and me.

With each step backward, the guys moved forward. I felt my back bump up against the bar counter. From the corner of my eye I saw that my brothers were also up against the bar. We were trapped. For a fleeting moment I thought the five might turn around and walk off.

After all, they'd already had their fun at our expense. But the guy directly in front of me quickly pulled both hands from his pockets and flipped open a knife. At the same time, his four buddies flipped open their knives as well. My reaction was instantaneous. I went into fighting mode. I was back in the *dojang* sparring with Master Kim. Time slowed down and I jumped up high with a flying roundhouse kick that knocked the knives from two of the closest attackers. My landing was precise. I was now facing the others. A front jump-kick knocked the knives from the second two, followed by a backward roundhouse kick to quickly disarm the last remaining attacker. I resumed my attack on the first two guys with a sidekick into the stomach of one, swiftly followed by a sidekick into the chest of the other. Maybe ten seconds had passed, enough to have put all five attackers on the ground. Steve and Rick joined in with their fists and the fight continued. My body was in constant motion, just as my teacher had taught us. The fight lasted no more than three minutes, and ended when the construction guys threw up their hands in submission. With the threat over, the fight stopped.

This was the first time I had used my Tae Kwon Do training outside the *dojang*. I found myself shocked at how effective it was. In my short lifetime, I had been in many fights, but I had never been able to dominate so easily and effortlessly. It was astonishing the way my trained body knew where it was vulnerable before my mind had consciously perceived an incoming punch. Blocking maneuvers, punches, flying kicks, over and over, in continuous motion—that's the basic fighting pattern of Tae Kwon Do. Although I'd used my training in self-defense, I was scared that this skill was too dangerous for someone with my background; I could easily kill someone without intending to.

I surveyed the scene and noticed blood on the floor. I checked my own body for a knife cut, but I was okay, as were my two brothers. Then I saw that one of our attackers had some serious, though non-life-threatening, cuts to his chest. Since I'd disarmed the men of their knives, I was puzzled over how one of them could have been cut. The bartender then told us the police were on their way, so we stepped outside the club to wait. Suddenly I heard "Look out!" I turned around and saw the guy who'd been cut in the chest holding a knife and charging toward me at full speed. One thing about Tae Kwon Do is that you learn to conserve your energy, and I had more than enough left to disarm this fellow again with a back roundhouse kick followed by a front jump-kick to his stomach and an uppercut to the chin that knocked him backward. I could hear the sound of his head hitting the pavement as he fell. He was knocked out cold.

During those few moments, police squad cars had swarmed around us and I was thrown immediately to the sidewalk and handcuffed. The police had arrived just in time to see me punching the guy, but not quickly enough to have seen him coming at me with the knife that was now lying on the ground. I tried explaining the sequence of events to an officer, but he threw me in a squad car anyway and whisked me away to the police station. Because witnesses at the scene identified both Steve and Rick as participants in the fight, they were detained shortly afterward and taken to the station as well.

At the precinct, the detective in charge was mostly concerned about the evidence of a knife attack perpetrated on—not *by*—my attacker. He told me that based upon what the police had witnessed, I would likely be arrested on charges of attempted murder. Their assumption was that I had cut the guy's chest using the knife that had been found outside the club. Steve, Rick, and I were being held together in an interrogation room for questioning. At sixteen, Rick was technically a juvenile, but he was being detained with us nonetheless. I pleaded with the detective to talk to the bartender and prayed that witnesses would come forward at the bar and tell the truth.

Hours went by at the police station while we waited for the detective to return from his investigation at the scene of the incident. I could hear policemen in the station talking on their radio about the fight, saying that witnesses had described me and my brothers as professional fighters. In my mind, I kept going over the fight inside the club, trying to understand how the guy might have been cut. I remembered seeing each of the knives fall to the ground as I knocked them out of the attackers' hands. An explanation eluded me.

Finally, the detective returned and told us that we were free to go. The guy's knife wounds were superficial. And more than one witness had confirmed our version of the events. Before releasing us, the detective said to me, "I better not catch you in another fight in this city."

I was shaken up over the whole episode and was especially concerned about the police warning. No one should have been cut in that fight. I grilled Steve and Rick about what they may have seen or done, but both of them denied having seen or done anything. Months later, after Rick joined the navy, he confessed to me that he had picked up one of the knives from the floor and cut one of the attackers during the scuffle.

After that fight, I never went into the Broadway Barn again. I also refused friends who pleaded with me to show off my martial arts skills. That kind of request made me uncomfortable. It labeled me a fighter, which could only lead to more trouble.

CHAPTER FORTY-ONE

A Man Who Can Take the Heat

At Frost Arnett, I excelled in the job of an adjustor. I knew firsthand what it was like to live in a household struggling to live from one paycheck to the next. Most people had the full intention of honoring their obligation, unlike my father, who had borrowed money never intending to pay it back. I had absolute freedom to negotiate reasonable payment terms within a person's ability to pay. I felt like I was helping people to work themselves out of a bad situation. In the office, two lists of the best adjustors were posted on the company bulletin board—one weekly, one monthly—and I was consistently in the top ten on both.

Prior to sitting down at our desks in the morning, all male employees hung their overcoats and suit jackets in the cloakroom. My only business jacket was a thin, black suit coat from a thrift shop. Once I'd saved enough money for a new one, I purchased a tan, single-breasted, light-wool sport coat that I loved. When I showed up for work in the new jacket the next day, I felt so proud of it that I decided to wear it for a while before hanging it up in the cloakroom. I noticed other employees looking my way and assumed they were admiring my brand-new sport coat. I wasn't aware that the boss had a firm rule against sport coats.

Mr. Martin came marching in my direction at a quick clip. He stopped in front of my desk, began wagging his index finger in my face, and said, "Who do you think you are—a used-car salesman? If you want to keep your job, you better get out of my office right now. And don't come back until you are wearing a suit."

Stunned, I couldn't speak. His voice was deep, his command firm, and his words bellowed out as if he were using a bullhorn.

"Go on, out of here!" he shouted, pointing his finger toward the door.

"But, Mr. Martin, I don't own a suit," I said.

The look on his face hinted at sympathy, but only for a moment. Meanwhile, all eyes and ears in the office were attending to our conversation.

Mr. Martin turned and glared at his fifty other employees, who instantly tucked their heads back down and resumed work at their telephones and tidy desks.

Now, Mr. Martin's expression showed maximum irritation. Nothing upset him more than an interruption of productivity. It was obvious that my sport coat had created a stir in the office. His eyebrows furrowed.

"Well, go buy a suit! That is what I pay you for!" he said, turning on his heel.

Embarrassed, I looked around the office, unsure of my next move. Several of my fellow adjusters were stealing glimpses at me. I snapped out of my momentary trance and left the office. I walked directly to the nearest men's clothing store and bought the cheapest suit on the rack. It was charcoal gray and cost seventy-five dollars. I didn't like the suit, but it would prove to be one of the wisest investments of my lifetime. I left the store wearing the ill-fitting suit, my other pants and jacket in a bag, and returned to work in less than an hour. I was determined not to allow my ego to interfere with a good-paying job.

Back in the office, during one of our two fifteen-minute breaks, a couple of the guys told me that I should have told the boss where he could stick the job. They "wouldn't have taken that kind of crap," they told me. I was surprised that they considered Mr. Martin's behavior something worth quitting their jobs over. In the army, I'd had to low-crawl underneath muddy barracks before morning light just because another soldier had been late falling into formation. Compared to that, this office interlude was nothing. Besides, I considered Mr. Martin a brilliant businessman and had no intention of quitting my job or doing anything to offend him. I knew I had a lot to learn from him and planned to be around long enough to take it all in. I suspected that my outwardly calm response to his reprimand might even enhance my standing with Mr. Martin because I'd proved to him that I was a man who could take the heat.

For the rest of the day, I made an effort to walk back and forth in front of his office so he'd know I was back on the job and dressed for the part.

Mr. Martin was a self-made multimillionaire who had worked his way up from the bottom. He'd started with nothing. I thought his obsessive and overbearing management style to be ineffective and outdated, but I understood his pride in having achieved great wealth on his own. He was living proof of the American dream. He wasn't a perfect role model—in many ways I found him to be an old-fashioned, cantankerous, and bigoted old man—but his weaknesses were my strengths. I could use my ability to get along with others to help my boss operate more efficiently. Once I saw the opportunity for me to move up in this company, I made the decision to use his organization as a stepping-stone.

With Mr. Martin, it was always about the money. To succeed in his company, all you had to do was to live by his rules and make the man money. He wasn't a complicated man when it came to running his business, and that was one of the incredible things I liked most about him. He didn't hide his agenda or talk abstractly. For example, his mission statement for all employees might be something like, "The mission of a company employee is to be prompt, professional, and productive at all times." Period. I could understand that. If you worked hard and made money for him, then he rewarded you without regard to your longevity within or loyalty to his company. Employees gained no advantage by playing politics with the boss, nor did they benefit because of their social and economic background, or because of which schools they'd attended. The way I saw it, his company provided a level playing field, which allowed me to compete for the best jobs without having to wait in line. I had a keen appreciation for this philosophy.

Six months after I was hired, Mr. Martin called me into his office and said he had a favor to ask of me. He had a valuable commercial client who was unhappy; he wanted me to restore this relationship for the company. "Can I count on you to do that?" he said. Naturally, I answered yes.

I took on the account, and within the first month, the client contacted Mr. Martin to congratulate him for the turnaround in both performance and relations. I didn't mind the extra work and found the task an easy one to accomplish. Subsequently, and to my surprise, Mr. Martin announced during an office meeting that I was one of the best employees in his company. His recognition of my performance in front of the other employees and managers enhanced my standing in the office. It also put me in the crosshairs of those who considered me to be a threat.

From then on, Mr. Martin used me as a troubleshooter to resolve rocky relationships with clients. In fact, salvaging client relationships had become my full-time job. I was effective in communicating with clients on the telephone, and I found the work easy and free of stress. Clients needed assurances that our company would perform in accordance with our contracts. My job was all about keeping clients happy. I kept copious notes of every phone discussion I had with them so I could refresh my memory in later conversations. I did my best to make every client feel as if they were the most important client we had.

Mr. Martin knew how to get the best out of me. Though his management style, and particularly his comments, could be caustic, everyone in his organization suffered equally. I was no stranger to abuse. But I could take as much heat as he dished out, and that advantage would catapult me ahead of all other employees.

CHAPTER FORTY-TWO

The Company You Keep

B y early summer, I'd been home for nearly a year since my discharge from the army. I had a secure, good-paying job where I was appreciated and learning things about running a business. I was still going to the University of Tennessee at night, although at the rate I was going, it would be two more years before I could graduate. Having so much time left before graduation made me restless, and I thought about it constantly.

I was also feeling discontented with Nashville. Somehow, no matter how hard I tried, I continually got swept up into its dark underbelly. That's where old friends hung out; that's where my brothers hung out. But what I didn't know then, and do know now, is that returning home to Nashville had been necessary for me, necessary for the final, painful shedding of my violent skin and old way of life. I just had a few last fights to go through first.

One weekend night in East Nashville, I attended a private party of about fifty with my older sister Faye and my brother Bracy. Faye had divorced her husband in the past year and had come to the party with her date, Terry, who had driven us in an old blue van. Except for some new faces, I knew most of the people there. I was outside on the front lawn with my date talking to friends when I heard Bracy call from inside the house, "Help me, Doug."

I ran into the house. Three guys, unknown to me, had pinned Bracy against the living room wall and were punching him with hard body blows. It took only seconds to break it up by putting myself between Bracy and the fighters. But the moment they realized that Bracy and I were brothers, the scuffle started up again as they decided to take on both of us. Once again, I relied upon my Tae Kwon Do training and quickly put an end to the fight. I regretted that furniture had gotten banged up—the television screen busted, lamps knocked to the floor, a coffee table broken in two.

"We'd better go," I told Bracy.

I located Faye outside. "We have to leave. There's going to be trouble," I said. My fighter's sense told me it wasn't over. Terry jumped in the van and started the engine.

The partygoers huddled together and watched as we climbed into the van. Suddenly, Bracy, who was still outside, shouted, "Quick, there's a gun!" Just as he jumped in and slammed the van door shut behind him, we heard the unmistakable sounds of gunfire. I leaped to cover my sister and my date, shoving them both to the floor. I could hear the hollow thumping and dinging of bullets penetrating the van as we sped away. After we had driven a safe distance, I sat up. I could see the light shining through the bullet holes in the van. We were safe but all pretty rattled. This was the kind of social interaction that I had not missed in Wisconsin or in Korea.

There were a number of fights and close calls that year, but I remember the last one well, not because it was any better or worse than any of the other fights, but because it was my last. I received a phone call on a spring night from my former brother-in-law, Wally, asking me to go with him to hear a country music band playing on Murfreesboro Road in East Nashville. Part of me wanted to go and have a good time, but Wally was a devious sort. I didn't trust him, so I said no. But he kept nagging me until finally I gave in. I told him I'd go on the condition that we leave the club no later than ten o'clock because I had to get up early the next day for work.

Later, at the club, I was on the dance floor when I noticed Wally having an argument with a patron. It was already nine-thirty, so I walked over and said, "We have to go."

As we were leaving, the guy who'd been arguing with Wally pitched his beer at both of us, with Wally getting the brunt of it because he was in the lead. Wally started to go after the guy, but I grabbed him and said, "Let's get out of here—*now*."

As we were exiting, because he couldn't leave it alone, Wally turned to the man and said, "Why don't you step outside?" Immediately I tried to override Wally's challenge and shouted to the guy, "Please don't, we do *not* want trouble."

We had almost reached Wally's car when I heard heavy footsteps coming out of the bar. I turned and saw seven angry-looking guys moving straight toward us. *It's always a pack*, I thought.

My martial arts training is all that saved us from an ugly beating. We were lucky that the fight stopped before anyone got seriously hurt. Wally, who'd stood passively by, was thrilled by what he'd seen and, all the way home, wanted to talk about it. But I wasn't listening. I strongly suspected that this had been a setup, that Wally had deliberately started the fight. He'd seen my Tae Kwon Do skills in action at the Broadway Barn months before. He had used me, I felt certain. As we drove back down Murfreesboro Road in Wally's black pickup, I thought about how I'd been hanging around with the wrong people and I needed to change that. I no longer lived in the housing projects, but you couldn't tell it by the company I kept. I made a promise to myself that I had fought my last fight.

Safe at home and in the quiet of bed, I realized that when the time was right I would have to move away from Nashville—for good.

CHAPTER FORTY-THREE

The Precipice of Change

After that night, I stayed away from all bars and nightclubs. I told Steve that he could no longer invite his friends over to our apartment. Like mine, Steve's friends were mostly from East Nashville, guys he'd met when he was living in the projects, which, for him, wasn't that long ago. He didn't agree with me that they were a bad influence, and this issue became a point of contention between us for a number of months.

But the bond between Steve and me was greater than any disagreement. We loved each other. That was a given. He continued to attend the university at night, which was giving him exposure to diverse people and possibilities. He was still working for the same company and had received a pay raise that made us equal in salary. I was proud of what he was accomplishing. I could see his world expanding. But his situation was fragile. His friends from the old neighborhood stayed in close contact with him and, whenever he was with them, he'd revert to his old ways. Ultimately, I knew that Steve couldn't live in both worlds. One day, he was going to have to choose. To my dismay, Steve made that choice in a way that created hardships for both of us.

I was at school one night when Steve threw a party at our place, inviting his friends from the housing projects. During the party, someone threw a beer bottle from our apartment balcony to the parking lot below. Thankfully, no one was injured and no property was damaged. When I arrived home, the security guard told me he'd had to break up the party with a threat to call the police. He was in the process of making a report to the manager, who would be on duty at eight o'clock the following morning. He was giving me a heads-up.

Steve was in the kitchen when I walked in. He was edgy and drunk. He said the beer hadn't intentionally been thrown from the balcony, that it had been an accident. I didn't think anything could be gained by discussing it then, so I went straight to bed, thinking that we had lost any chance of renewing our lease on the apartment we had been in for eleven months.

First thing the next morning, I went to the apartment manager's office. The owners of the building had strict rules regarding tenant behavior, and there was a waiting list of people wanting to move in. Plus, the manager had been unhappy with the frequent gatherings in our unit and she was just waiting for a reason to kick us out.

When I entered her office, the manager's anger was palpable. To make the situation less uncomfortable for both of us, I volunteered to vacate the apartment before the end of the week. Steve and I moved out of Capitol City Towers and into a two-bedroom apartment on Belmont Avenue on the west side of town. The apartment complex was in a nice neighborhood, but not as nice or new or convenient as where we'd been.

Steve and I settled into a new routine of school and work—a twenty-minute drive downtown for each of us. Now that we both had to commute, we had less time for play, which I considered a good thing. Perhaps to cheer us up after our eviction, we decided to get a dog from the local pound, a five-year-old, mixed-breed golden retriever. We named her Comet because she ran so fast, and when she ran, her long golden hair reminded us of a comet streaking across the sky. She was such a good dog and immediately became the best friend of everyone in the apartment complex, including the manager.

By that time, Steve had saved enough to buy his own car, a red '62 VW bug, and I was driving my red '63 VW fastback, purchased shortly after the road trip to California. Comet learned to recognize the sounds of our respective car engines and came running across lawns and parking lots to dive into our passenger side windows as we approached the apartment every evening. We left a window open in our first-floor apartment while we were gone, so she could come and go as she pleased. She behaved responsibly and was an unusually smart and loyal dog. Comet was the kind of dog every boy and man dreams of owning. She was my first dog since Blackie when I was seven.

Steve's behavior changed dramatically with the move to the new apartment. The incident that got us kicked out of the Capitol Towers made him realize how his actions had consequences for the both of us. He seemed more positive and eager now that he had his own automobile. An added plus was the fact that Comet gave us both reason to look forward to coming home every night. For the first time since arriving home from Korea, I was optimistic that I would be able to help all my brothers break through the social barriers that plague victims of generational poverty. Steve was on the precipice of change. He had broken off relations with his old friends from East Nashville. He seemed to enjoy his new life and it showed in the way he dressed and the language he used. His behavior had changed as well, and he made new friends at school. There was reason for my optimism that Steve was on the verge of breaking through the social barrier, that hidden ceiling that permanently condemns poverty victims to repeat the cycle.

CHAPTER FORTY-FOUR

"I'll Take It"

I n the years when I was living on South Seventh Street, whenever I was feeling overwhelmed by what was going on in the
projects or inside my own home, I turned to work. At twenty-
two, I was making use of that same survival skill. I was doing away
with an unsettling social life and turning my attention exclusively to
school and work—and resolving to work harder at both. I became
one of the first to arrive in the office in the morning and one of the
last to leave at night. I was consistently a top performer for the
company and had decided to push for a promotion to one of the
company's branch offices. Transferring to a new school would not
be a problem.

In August, almost a year after having been hired at Frost Arnett,
my opportunity arose. At our weekly staff meetings, Mr. Martin routinely briefed us on the company's profitability. This day, as usual, he
began by expressing his disgust for those who had failed to produce
results. As he often did, he used me as an example of how one person

can make a difference. As a great storyteller from the old school, he would elaborate and embellish on this theme. As Mamma Pearl would say, "He could spin a yarn a mile long." Being singled out made me wince, but getting recognized publicly by Mr. Martin was a prerequisite to moving up in his company. That's how it worked.

On this particular morning, he moved on to discuss the status of the branch offices located in the Southeast. Specifically, he addressed the fact that his Atlanta branch had been losing money.

"Now, you take this Wallace boy here," Mr. Martin said. "If he wasn't in college, I would send him straight to Atlanta to manage that office. I bet that boy could turn that office around."

No sooner were the words out of his mouth than I jumped up from my chair and announced, "Mr. Martin, I will take you up on that offer."

With raised eyebrows, he told me to meet him in his office at three o'clock that afternoon, four hours hence.

The public interchange had created quite a reaction in the office. Many of my coworkers started weighing in. Some believed that Mr. Martin had been making a hypothetical point only, not an actual job offer. Others doubted that Mr. Martin would ever fire the existing branch manager in Atlanta in order to replace him with *me*, by which they meant a neophyte. Larry, my original trainer, laughed and said, "You called that old man's bluff, Wallace."

Actually, I had taken Mr. Martin quite literally. But, at minimum, whether he'd meant to or not, he'd opened a door to a possibility that had taken hold of me. I didn't know the phrase *carpe diem* then, but this was a seize-the-day moment if there ever was one. My simple strategy was to make it as difficult as possible for Mr. Martin to squirm out of his pronouncement. I had nothing to lose.

At three o'clock sharp, I walked into Mr. Martin's office and he motioned to a chair in front of his desk. Instead of sitting behind it, as I expected, he came over and stood directly in front of me, so close that I could see the ceiling light reflected in his black, spit-shined shoes. Even though I was seated, he didn't tower over me; he was a short man. He wore his pants high-waisted, about six inches below his chest. His stomach was large and round, yet his clothes fit him well, giving him a distinguished appearance. I couldn't help but admire the quality of his suit—light gray with faint pinstripes—and I wondered if I would ever be able to afford a suit like that.

Mr. Martin peered down at me from below his round-rimmed glasses. I'd come prepared with a notepad and had printed at the top in large block letters, "ATLANTA PROMOTION—MEETING WITH MR. MARTIN." I had decided to lead with assumption.

Neither of us said anything for a long while.

"So you are willing to quit school for this job?" he said.

"Yes, sir," I said. To myself I was saying, *Keep your mouth shut. Let him do the talking.* I looked downward at my pad, poised with my fountain pen as though ready to write down my instructions for the Atlanta move. More silence. His eyes bore down on me. I did not want to look him in the eye lest my uncertainty betray itself.

As though I were making a checklist, on my notepad I entered the task, "Withdraw from school."

"Of course, I can't make you a manager," he said. "I already have a manager in Atlanta."

Had he just slammed the door shut? I looked up at him and allowed my disappointment to show. More silence still. I could hear him breathing.

"You think you could make a difference down there, son?"

My response was instantaneous. "Yes, sir!" I said. The army had taught me those words so well, and my posture was straight.

"Well," he dragged it out. "I could make you an *assistant* manager."

I nodded my head perfunctorily in order to conceal my elation at the direction this conversation was going, and I continued to let him do all the talking for fear I'd screw it up otherwise.

"Of course, I couldn't pay you the salary of a manager," Mr. Martin added.

Now, I knew we were really getting somewhere. I didn't say a word.

"I'll pay you twenty-five thousand per year and that's it," he said. That doubled my current salary.

"I'll take it," I said.

I stood up and extended my hand to seal the deal. I looked him confidently in the eye and said, "Thank you, Mr. Martin. I will not let you down."

Walking out of his office, if a guy can glow, I was glowing.

I'll never know for sure whether or not Mr. Martin had seriously considered me for a transfer to Atlanta. All I know is that I liked the outcome. My coworkers, however, were not so pleased. Some of the more senior employees, all good employees, had been waiting for years to get an assignment to one of the branch offices. They weren't about to concede any ground to me. Putting up with a work environment under Mr. Martin's watchful eye had been part of the price they'd been paying to win such a choice assignment. Several employees resented being skipped over in favor of the youngest and newest adjustor in the office.

So, for the rest of the week I had to deal with the complex reactions to my promotion. I did my best to be respectful during my remaining few days.

One more time, I was leaving Nashville and all the violence behind, hoping to start a new life. Hope dies hard among the faithful. The irresistible nature of hope is the idea that all is not lost; that things will get better. That's what keeps driving me—the belief that if I try hard enough, if I keep pushing hard enough, then God will show me the way—that everything will be all right. No one promised that it would all happen at once. It's a long-haul journey, and the move to Atlanta was part of that. The moment I drove passed the city limits of Nashville, the tension in my muscles eased.

CHAPTER FORTY-FIVE

Atlanta

I fell in love with Atlanta at first sight. In 1972, it was already an amazing city, poised to be the regional center of the South, a city in the early stages of explosive growth. Its motto was "city too busy to hate." I thought it remarkable that Atlanta not only acknowledged the existence of hate, but proclaimed itself above it. On my first visit, I could feel the energy of the place, and its youthfulness. It had a shine. There was no rough entry. It felt right, like a good place for me.

Steve had decided he wanted to make the move with me, so I drove on ahead, and found us a two-bedroom apartment in the northeast section of the city. I left my car there and flew back to Nashville. We rented a U-Haul truck, loaded it up with our personal belongings from Belmont Avenue, and then headed to our new home. Saying goodbye to Mom was never easy for me—I felt like I was abandoning her. I felt like I was abandoning Comet too. I hadn't been able to find an apartment that allowed dogs. Mom had agreed to take her for the time being. When our first lease expired, our plan was to find a place that accepted pets. Leaving Comet behind was almost as hard as leaving Mom.

The first week in Atlanta, I applied for the fall semester at Georgia State University, which had a night school program and was located downtown, only five blocks from my new office. I could walk to school directly after work.

The Frost Arnett Company was located downtown on the fifth floor of the landmark sixteen-story Healey Building. The Healey was a contemporary to the Flatiron Building in New York City, except its pointed arches and stone facade embellished with terra-cotta made it seem more elegant. It stood directly across the street from the old federal courthouse.

The Atlanta office, which employed about twenty people, was considerably smaller than the company headquarters in Nashville. The office manager, Jim Niedert, was in his early forties, and the sales manager, James Smith, in his mid-sixties. I was the new assistant office manager, reporting to Jim Niedert. Working for the company in Atlanta was radically unlike working in the Nashville office. The atmosphere was casual and the employees not nearly as disciplined. The desks were not in perfect alignment, nor the men all dressed in white shirts. My initial thought upon seeing the office for the first time was that Mr. Martin would not get a moment's sleep if he had any idea what was going on in Atlanta.

The sales manager showed me around and filled me in on the status of things. Personally, I liked Mr. Smith, but I didn't like his negative attitude and the fact that he held a grudge against the home office. He told me that he'd been betrayed by Mr. Martin, who had reneged on a promise of an equity interest in the Atlanta office. My opinion was that Mr. Smith's attitude was the real problem. Salary, not equity, is given as a reward for a job well done. To earn equity, Mr. Smith would have had to contribute something beyond what he was already being paid to do. From what I could tell, his resentment was doing more harm than good to the Atlanta branch.

A few weeks after my arrival, the office manager, Jim Niedert, suffered a back injury, which required surgery and left him temporarily
disabled and unable to return to work. The Nashville office promoted
me—provisionally—to office manager. Two significant promotions
back-to-back felt like sailing with a strong wind at my back. Although
the promotion was only temporary, it enhanced my status within the
office and gave me the authority to make some improvements, starting with the department most responsible for producing income.

As a manager, I modeled my operational plan on Mr. Martin's. In
Atlanta, there were no existing procedures for measuring employee
production, so I adopted the daily management reports we'd used at
the Nashville office. I also randomly monitored the outbound calls
and conducted half-hour training sessions with the staff every day in
order to build their communication skills on the telephone.

With these and a few other straightforward changes, the office
improved from a loss in the prior month to a gain of twenty-five
thousand dollars in the next. The division manager in charge of all
branch offices called me personally and wanted to know how I'd been
able to turn a profit so rapidly. I told him that I had implemented the
procedures I had learned in Nashville. He loved my response and said
that Mr. Martin would be pleased to hear that.

As a reward to myself, I decided to purchase a new suit from an
upscale department store in Atlanta called Muse's. I'd heard that
the men's department sold the most expensive suits in town. The
moment I walked in, I knew it was the place where I wanted to buy
my clothing. I tried on several suits and decided upon a light-gray suit
with subtle stripes. I'm color-blind to shades of red and green, so the
salesman helped me to pick out a shirt and tie to go with the suit, as
well as a belt, socks, and a new pair of shoes. I left the store owning a
suit of the quality that Mr. Martin was wearing on the day I received
my promotion. It looked very, very good.

Soon after, I purchased two more suits from Muse's—one navy-
blue pinstripe, the other dark-gray wool. The clothes were an invest-
ment. Along the way, I had learned that you dress for the job you
want. You spare no expense.

CHAPTER FORTY-SIX

Change Begins at Home

Steve found a job downtown, just a few blocks from my office, working at a department store as a sales clerk. He was a great communicator, which served him well as a salesman. Watching from the outside, it seemed like he was at a high point in his life. He had come far. He'd adjusted smoothly to living in Atlanta and was instantly popular at Georgia State University, where he'd enrolled as a sophomore. He was at the top of his game, I thought. He had that special look about him. I have an image of him leaving our apartment on his way somewhere on an autumn Sunday afternoon with a pretty girl tucked under each arm.

In mid-December, I received a phone call from Mom saying that Comet had run away. She told us that Comet had spent most of her days gazing out the living room window as though she were anticipating the arrival of our two Volkswagens at any moment. Then one day Comet simply jumped through the glass and made her getaway. Mom thought that Comet might be somewhere in Nashville looking for us. Very upset, Steve and I made the drive from Atlanta to search for her. We drove up and down the streets—in East Nashville and also across the river where she'd lived with us—calling her name for hours at a time. Friends came and helped us look, but we found no trace of her. We gave up after four days. The long ride back to Atlanta was awful. I hoped there was a chance she'd show up back at my mother's, but she never did.

During our brief stay in Nashville, I noticed that Steve and Rick spent a lot of time discussing our "bachelor pad" in Atlanta. Steve had always been close to Rick and was encouraging him to join us. But Rick was still in high school, a senior at East Nashville, with only a semester to go before graduating. As I had with Steve, who'd stuck it out and received his diploma, I encouraged Rick to see it through. After he graduated, we could talk about his future plans, I told him. As his older brother, I held some sway but didn't kid myself that it was anything but tenuous.

A few days after Steve and I arrived back in Atlanta, Rick called to tell us that he had dropped out of high school and wanted to move in with us right away. I was stunned and tried to convince him to go back. I was opposed to his coming to Atlanta without having graduated. But there was no changing his mind. Steve argued that Rick should be given the opportunity to get away from Nashville. He thought that Rick had a better chance of making it in Atlanta, as Steve had. He was strongly in favor of allowing him to join us as a roommate—he had offered to share his room with Rick. Since he was paying half of our apartment expenses, Steve felt, and rightly so, that he was entitled to a substantial say in the matter.

As his older brother, my say had always carried a little more weight than Steve's. Perhaps for that reason, to compensate, I agreed—with apprehension—that Rick could join us. I decided I would work with Rick as much as I had with Steve to help him make the transition from the only life he'd ever known to the better, more hopeful life that we were experiencing now in Atlanta. The mindset of the poor can be, and usually is, a prison. If I could just help to put a crack in that prison wall, maybe some light could get in, as it had for me.

Rick moved in over the Christmas holidays and promptly found a job as a truck driver close to home. Like his brothers—Bracy, Steve, and me—Rick was good at finding work. He told us that he planned to take the GED exam and then join us at Georgia State once he was eligible for admission. Within a few weeks, though, it became obvious that Rick was not going to take the GED or enter college. He reminded me of Bracy in that way. Rick's primary interest was in having a good time and going places with his big brother Steve, and this created a situation at home that began to unravel the status quo.

Steve was only twenty and had been free of East Nashville for only a short time. He'd been living with me a little more than a year. He was teachable but still vulnerable to the pull of the streets. He needed more time to adjust to the social and educational challenges that confront someone who comes from the bottom and tries to make it in mainstream America. From my own experience, I knew this transition to be painful, which is why so few ever make it. As for Rick, he was only twelve when I left home for the Job Corps in Wisconsin. He was a streetwise kid who had learned to make his own way through life without help from anyone. Rick was even more raw and rough around the edges than Steve. When he moved in with us in Atlanta, he brought with him, through no fault of his own, the dreadful baggage of the housing projects.

Steve had been planning to enroll for the winter semester at Georgia State, but at the last minute decided not to. He told me that he was taking a semester off. We had several arguments over his decision. Eventually, he quit his job as a salesman and starting driving trucks again. I continued to talk to him and also to Rick about their education, about starting to think about what they wanted to do with their lives. But they saw my concern as unwelcome interference. Slowly, Steve returned to his old ways. He and Rick hung out in the local bars and nearby parks, often getting into fights with other street toughs. Their daily lives were focused on the consumption of alcohol and any form of activity that involved a twelve-pack of beer.

Late-night parties at our apartment became commonplace. My living situation was untenable for me, so I often stayed with a girlfriend. I had no choice but to talk to my brothers about how they needed to change their ways. They told me that they were both having the greatest time of their lives and didn't want to let the joy of the moment go. They thought there was plenty of time to go to college. Their new motto was "live for the here and now." They had no concept of adding a linear dimension to their lives, of taking one step after another and actually gaining some traction that could take them somewhere, somewhere different and better. We were brothers, but we were worlds apart. I had to face the reality that I was powerless over their choices and behavior; I'd lost any influence I may have had. As a team of two, they put it to me bluntly, "Stop trying to run our lives." I had to let go.

The three of us shared the apartment for about seven months. Toward the end of the lease, we decided to go our separate ways. Steve and Rick got an apartment of their own; they asked me for money for the rent deposit, and I gave it to them. I found a nice one-bedroom apartment on Biscayne Drive, two blocks off Peachtree Road, in the small community of Buckhead. It was an up-and-coming area for young professionals, and only a ten-minute drive from work and school.

Making the decision to part from Steve and Rick was a hard choice and another defining moment in my life. There would be no turning back to how it used to be. I was glad to be away from the chaos and alcohol, happy to have a place of my own, but I continued to worry about the two of them. For most of our lives, we'd been inseparable buddies, a tight-knit band of brothers, in Stewart County and then in Nashville. But we'd gone our different ways. I knew I was doing what was best for me, but it was painful to acknowledge that we were growing apart.

CHAPTER FORTY-SEVEN

Opportunity Knocks

I n April 1973, less than a year after moving to Atlanta, I was made permanent office manager at Frost Arnett. The profits had continued to climb. I had one overriding strategy that served me well: *Keep Mr. Martin happy.* As long as I maintained profitability and kept the clients satisfied, I could count on Mr. Martin giving me ample time to learn the fundamentals of business management.

I was working ridiculously long and hard hours at work, managing not only the customer service staff but the administrative staff as well. Standing instructions to my secretary included interrupting me anytime one of the company's top ten clients called. For any clients not on that list, I made a personal commitment to return their calls within fifteen minutes. I created a daily performance report that provided a general overview of each department and also a report of the backlog of items left unfinished at the end of the day. The last thing I did before leaving each night was to review these reports and plan the next day accordingly. In the morning, I arrived early in order to prepare the work assignments for the day and, in the evening, left in time for school, which began at seven o'clock.

The officer manager position brought with it a welcome increase in salary and bonuses, which made living alone more affordable and which meant I could send more money home. But I had no intention of remaining long-term at Frost Arnett, and never had. What I still wanted most was a license to practice law.

Occupying the top three floors of the Healey Building, the very building where I worked, was a small law school called the Woodrow Wilson College of Law. A month after my promotion, to learn more about the school, I went upstairs and introduced myself to the director of admissions, a woman named Ruth Sills, whom I'd seen a number of times in the elevator. She was an imposing, highly competent, smart woman in her fifties. I asked her to have lunch with me one day soon and she accepted. On a weekday in May, the spring sun warm and the air fresh, we walked to a popular nearby Greek restaurant. During lunch, I let her know that I'd been interested in law since I was a child. She gave me an overview of the school and its program, which consisted of classes four hours a night, five days a week, year-round, no summer breaks, for thirty-six months—in other words, the kind of hard work I was used to. The college had a student body of about three hundred and it was one of the oldest law schools in the state. Ruth Sills had worked there for the past twenty-five years and knew all the judges and politicians in Atlanta who'd graduated from Woodrow Wilson. I realized that she held considerable influence regarding admissions.

At Georgia State I'd been taking courses in criminal law and also civil procedures. That summer, I enrolled in a juvenile law class, which I found exceptionally compelling given my background with teenage toughs. In class one day, early in the semester, I learned something that had been completely unknown to me. Applicants for the Georgia Bar Association were required to have a law degree, but not necessarily an undergraduate degree. All the GBA required was a minimum of two years of college. The professor then informed us that there were three law schools in Atlanta that accepted applications for admission for students who did not have a college degree. One of them was Woodrow Wilson College of Law. I was dumbfounded that I hadn't known this before. I didn't regret any of my time spent as an undergraduate, but getting a degree at nighttime is laborious and ponderously slow. I had been trudging and still had a ways to go. If I could bypass the classes remaining and go straight to law school, well, that was the road for me.

The next morning I called Ruth Sills and asked her to lunch again. This time I told her everything—my family background, the Job Corps, UW Eau Claire, the army, and my lifelong ambition to become an attorney. I then told her that I wanted to apply for admission in the fall. But the fall class began in only five weeks, she told me, and admissions for this coming term had been closed for a year. I pleaded my case. Reluctantly, because she didn't want to raise false hope, she agreed to speak to the Dean about me. She said she'd call me back in the afternoon to let me know the outcome. I could tell that she was doing this as a special favor to me and I felt confident that she would make her best effort. It was in her hands.

Later that day she called. She told me that I had an appointment to meet with the board of directors at ten o'clock the next morning. They weren't making any promises, she added, but they were willing to hear me out.

CHAPTER FORTY-EIGHT

A Dream Comes True

I skipped school that night and stayed up well past midnight creating a portfolio of all my records—Job Corps, GED diploma, college, military, employment—records that I kept in a cheap, brown valise, which I still have today. I also wrote a personal statement. The words didn't come easily, but I managed to write a succinct two pages.

The next morning my nerves were shattered. I got up before five a.m., riding high on adrenaline. I feared a stark, outright, cut-and-dried rejection by the board. But at the same time, from that place deep within, I felt that everything was going to be all right. I had prepared and all I could do was give it my best shot.

At precisely 9:55, I walked into the admissions office on the sixteenth floor, wearing my dark-gray wool suit with a pair of fine-leather black shoes and carrying a smooth black leather briefcase.

Smiling, Ruth Sills came out to greet me in the lobby. She ushered me into a small boardroom where four men, also in suits and sharply dressed, were seated at a polished mahogany conference table. All were lawyers and two were retired superior court judges. They introduced themselves and pointed to a vacant chair. I remember the youngest among them, a lawyer in his forties, shook my hand so firmly it almost hurt; I squeezed right back, matching his intensity with my own and making eye contact with him. Ruth Sills had since left the room.

The interview lasted fifteen minutes, no more. Each of the gentlemen was curious about my background and asked a lot of questions about my current work. I'd assumed I'd have to argue my case— why they should consider making an exception in the admissions policy for me—but none of the men seemed interested in any kind of monologue from me. As I sensed the meeting coming to an end, I reached into my briefcase and pulled out the portfolios that I had assembled and handed each board member a copy. I asked them to please review my personal statement and the contents of my folder before making their final decision.

I took the elevator down to my office on the fifth floor and waited. In less than an hour, Ruth Sills, Director of Admissions for Woodrow Wilson College of Law, called to tell me that I had been admitted to the fall class of 1973.

Fifteen years before, when I was eight years old, the principal of my two-room schoolhouse had told me, as the poorest boy in my class, that college and law school were unlikely options for me. Establish realistic goals, he'd said. His words would have crushed most boys' dreams forever. But I was lucky. They didn't come near to where my soul resides.

Epilogue

I told the Frost Arnett that I planned to attend law school at night, and it was agreed that I could continue as office manager. It was an ideal, well-paying job that gave me invaluable experience in managing a business. The GI Bill paid the full cost of my law school tuition, so I was still able to help Mom.

On the first day of law school, the professor began class with the following statement: "Look to your left; and now look to your right. One of the people on either side of you will drop out of law school before your class graduates." *And I won't be one of them,* I thought to myself. Then he added, "Only one-third of the students who graduate will pass the bar exam." That got my attention. My goal was to become an attorney, not just to graduate from law school. The professor's comment captured the real purpose for my being there. What I was after was the license to practice law. I felt nervous and wondered if I would make it. I had more than three thousand hours of class time to go.

Three years later, on the first try, I passed the Georgia bar exam during my final semester in law school. I left my day job, lucrative as it was, and opened my own practice in Atlanta immediately following graduation. Mamma Pearl, my grandmother Wallace, had lived long enough to see me graduate.

A year after passing the bar, I bought my mother a spacious three-bedroom house with a wide front porch. It was surrounded by mature elms on an acre of land and had plenty of room for a garden.

My mother had divorced my father, who lived to be sixty-nine after finding sobriety toward the end of his life. I have long since forgiven my father for the harm he did to us, especially to my brothers and sisters. But the pain is never far away. My three brothers, Bracy, Steve, and Rick, lived hard lives, and none of them lived to be as old as my father. Bracy and Rick both died in their forties, Steve at age fifty. I believe that alcoholism—a family disease—contributed to their early deaths.

When my father was dying, I was still too angry to visit him. Although we came close to blows, I never did physically fight him, for which I am grateful. He's buried in Stewart County next to his father, in a churchyard in Big Rock.

As of this writing, my mother is eighty-four. When asked about the past, she simply says, "It was a pretty rough life."

I now own some land in different parts of the country, and one of my properties is a twenty-acre ranch on which I grow multiple vegetable gardens, like the ones my mother used to plant. Like she did, I can a lot of my vegetable crop for the winter. When I'm there, I often think of my grandfather Wallace—Papa Jim—and his five-acre farm that, from my earliest memories, was and remains an inspiration to me. To this day, along with my three dogs Alphonzo, Alfredo, and Mollie, I have chickens, goats, peacocks, and sheep. They keep me in touch with my roots in Stewart County, which is still one of the most beautiful places on earth, with its woods and creeks and hills. Tobacco is still grown there.

My land and properties are something that I own, but they don't own me. I'm not attached to any of them as a form of security. They could be gone tomorrow. Perhaps because my childhood family was landless and itinerant, I had no contact with any sense of security until I learned that everything I needed was in my heart. I learned this on the road through the woods that night in Potneck when God put a floor under all my sadness and fears and uncertainties. I don't pretend to know who or what God is. But I do believe in a fundamental innocence and presence of spirit and light inside and surrounding all of us. I believe that what I experienced on that nighttime road—which remains as fresh today as it was forty-eight years ago—happens to a lot of people, in different ways, every single day, in the ordinary miracle of just being, or in the quiet of prayer, or in the silence of meditation. I believe this taste of inner peace and love is possible for everyone, in every moment.

Looking back, I see so clearly how often, throughout my boyhood, I was touched by random acts of kindness that helped to shape me into the man I am today. And random acts of violence and ignorance played just as powerful a role in making me who I am.

The divine sparks that have lighted my way have been both ferocious and glorious. I am grateful for it all. And, for me, gratitude itself is a prayer.

Omnia bene evadent.
Everything will be all right.